-

c

o

p

e

For more information, find CCM at:

http://copingmechanisms.net

A SHADOW MAP

AN ANTHOLOGY BY
SURVIVORS OF
SEXUAL ASSAULT

EDITED BY
JOANNA C. VALENTE

For all survivors

FORWARD BY
JOANNA C. VALENTE

What does it mean to survive? We say we survive a traumatic event if we are still alive; better yet, if we are able to get beyond the pain, feel hope and contentment, and allow ourselves to love and be loved. But surviving also means living with the pain, not truly escaping the memories of a trauma. To survive sexual assault is a life-long journey. It means you survived the most brutal of physical and psychological violations while simultaneously surviving the death of the self, or your prior identity. It changes you. It changes how you trust, how you love.

Sometimes it feels like you never survived at all.

I never expected to curate an anthology focused on writing by sexual assault survivors. When I decided to spearhead the project, it surprised me to realize an anthology like this had never been done before—but it also wasn't entirely shocking. Sexual assault isn't taken seriously, not even in 2017—many survivors are often doubted, or told to "get over it," as if you can easily forget what happened.

The project was inspired by—sadly—our currently political climate—and most notably, by Donald Trump's unfortunate statement, "grab her by the pussy." Like many, I was outraged. I was humiliated that the American public supports someone like Trump—and that many don't see what was wrong with his comment—or thought it was just "locker room talk," not abusive, objectifying comments toward women. This was the moment I realized we, as writers, need to fight back. We need to use our language as protest. Change does not come without protest, without a movement—and movements historically start with language—with others uniting across the same belief.

Growing up, I always wanted to be a painter. Most people don't know this about me. I would spend hours drawing and painting, obsessing over the obscure details of artists' lives, recreating famous paintings (like Andy Warhol's soup cans when I was 12), and it wasn't until my teens that I seriously began writing; even then, I never thought I would become a writer whose work largely reflects a journey of self-discovery post-sexual assault and abortion. But then again, no one can really tell us the future. Humans can barely understand the present moment they're in—which is half the beauty of being alive, because everything is a possibility.

No one grows up thinking—or assuming—they'll be assaulted. No child assumes they won't have ownership over their body— or even truly understands what ownership entails—or how hard it is have possession over your needs, wants, and ability to make choices.

Rape is a violation of one's body.

Rape is a violation of one's ownership of their body.

Rape is the violation of consent, of being able to fully make an engaged choice.

When I was 20, I was raped. I was raped by a man I knew, a man I was briefly dating, a man I trusted, a man who was an artist in his community. I was raped more than once. At the time, I didn't want to accept what happened to me. When it happened the first time, I was asleep. I didn't know what to think of this in the moment—even when the man said he "hoped he hadn't just raped me." I stayed quiet. I never told my friends. I didn't know how, especially since I didn't "fight back" although I knew I never consented either. When it happened the second time, and I said no and I tried to fight back, it was harder for me to ignore. I confronted my abuser once, who told me I was crazy, and then never spoke to him again. I never pressed charges—because I didn't think it was possible—and there wasn't any evidence. I hadn't gone to the hospital after it happened. I merely went to bed.

While I've written essays and poetry about those experiences, I've never written about the time another man assaulted me. When I said I wasn't interested in sex and he asked if he could "stick it in a little," I froze and he had sex with me. Or the various times men touched my bodies in ways I wasn't comfortable at bars or at parties, readings, or coffee shops. It happened so often I became desensitized to unwanted touch—believing it was just how people are, that it was okay. I dealt with it by not believing I could have ownership over my own body. I wanted my body to go far way, just be a brain somewhere laying in the sunlight.

There was no pivotal moment for me that made me realize my body was my own, that no one had a right to it but me. I am still on my journey of self-discovery and survival—navigating a complicated world of murky turmoil—even, and most especially, within the literature community. All of the infighting within the community itself has been triggering and destabilizing for many.

For me, as a survivor, I can say now more than ever, we need to support each other, create spaces where survivors can speak and live without fear and disbelief. Is a space ever truly safe? I don't know. I would like to believe it is possible to create safe spaces, but in order to do that, we must always question our biases, our privileges, our own entitlements. We must move forward with kindness and compassion for each other.

No one is perfect—which means we can't expect our survivors to be perfect humans either—and disbelieve someone's story because we simply don't like them or don't know them. There is no "right" or perfect survivor. We are all survivors, and we are doing our best, even if it doesn't seem to be someone else's "best." Survivors are people you know, people you love—they have your face: They are women, men, people who identify in the LGBTQIA community. They are human. Rape knows no bounds or gender—and abusers are people we love, people in our communities, people we often would never suspect.

Now is the time to unite with each other, with our words, and rally. If we don't, the divide will only widen and that will be the real death of us all. I believe in you, in us. I know we can do the hard work and cross that bridge in the far distance, where the ocean howls, where the sun and moon shine in unison.

Always with love,

Joanna C. Valente
Editor

LYNN
MELNICK

Landscape with Smut and Pavement

At night I hallucinate the grunting discord

which leapt from a human body as he destroyed mine.
That very month, I obliterated a beetle on a shiny walkway.

That month was November.

I think they are all out to get me,
all the insects in their armor.

Some folks like to use the word *slut*, even with children.

I am holding all my blood in vials on my lap.

The splatter is delicate.
I guess I am bleeding all over the scenery.

I was born in November.

But you want to hear about the clean stretch of pavement
where a beetle once lived

or the surrounding archways that were the kind of architecture
that bodies who have been treated gently like to enjoy.

The kempt lawn was always kempt.
I was disparaged on that terrain.

I was smut.
The rest was burnished.

(First published in *A Public Space*)

One Sentence About Los Angeles

I've been trying to plant a palm in every garden
I slink through

using this intoxicating body I lucked into
some years after I first arrived

in the desert in a Datsun
with a commonplace finch in the back bench seat with me

and, while you're probably waiting for metaphors
because you know that's the most respectable skill I have

this is not a story about cages
and it sure isn't a story about wings

and, while you are probably waiting for confession
because you think that's what I've been doing here all along

this is not a story of how my body was first held down
before I'd even hit double digits

on a dingy carpet whose fibers are still
on my tongue, whose burn to my cheek I didn't even notice

amid the more traumatic injuries

until later I saw photos
because I couldn't look in the mirror

until the 21ˢᵗ century
but this, all of this, the rape and the allegory

and the skinny palms sheltering no one:

this is the story of how I got to live

in a city that had run one course and needed
another, roots humping

up the walkways so even sober we stumbled
toward the slowing cars which is what happens to girls

who grow up with all that poetry and carpet
in their mouths but remember

(I almost forgot to tell you)

I lived

in a desert
where palms are signposts of water, not the want of it.

(First published in *APR*)

Some Ideas for Existing in Public

I think you should grip your dick through your jeans and
        ask me

if I can handle it because you know I can, right?
I'm here for you.

                I think you should overtake me at a bus bench
and invite me to sit on your face.

I think you should track me down
the block and clarify how you'd like to split my slit open

until I pass out.

(Once, as a kid, I was balancing on a ledge
all morning thinking no one

could see me until a man walked by and captured my chin in his
        grip
and called me *pretty*.)

I think you should screw me sideways right here on the
    sidewalk
like you said you might like to screw me

sideways before you took off
past the cop who said it's pointless to prove the crime so

come on, sure
screw me sideways, and why just sideways, why not all ways?
Why not diagonal?

          I think you should whistle so loud at my fat ass
that I jump like a stray rodent and you couldn't be more cor-
rect, it is a shame

my fat ass is walking away

from you because why is it walking away from you?
Why am I walking away from you? Why am I here on the side-
walk?

I'm yours.

(First published in *The Awl*)

LAUREN
SAMBLANET

a crying woman

was nine years old
        the first time   that i can remember
    was tripping on shrooms
        when i told
                was six years old

    was repressed   was fucked by a man and a boy child
                was five years old

        was tripping on shrooms when i told ben
                was ripped apart

        was too narrative
was nineteen years old   when forced anally
was ripped open
        was blood let

was weeping on shrooms in ben's bed   was held
        was one year old

                blood let

OMOTARA JAMES

The Talk

we never had the talk
about the birds or the bees or the boys
who chased me

throbbing, through the hallways of school,
past the combination lockers and open rooms

where i sprinted for my life, turning right
sometimes left, for the atrium, but they
could always find the line to my scent,

an invisible thread, i could feel the vibrations
the treads of their soles

scuff 'cross the linoleum
floors of my virginity,
except i didn't know that word then, only

the muscular friction of their clumsy hands
over then under the brown sash

of the Brownies uniform
we were made to wear, every Tuesday and Thursday
something about school spirit   i used to love to run

to chase the blood in my thighs
— not the boys   they preferred us still

beneath them, swollen with the silence
of seedlings desperate to sprout
as they took turns reaping us

digging their fingers into our soft, brown flesh
breaking in our brand new breasts

and twisting our nipples (hard)
like they were turning the earth, like it was their rite
to pull us through that passage

breathless
still, I recall the first prod

the first pinch of my fat in their flat fingers,
the surprise of his nails like ice,
like the first frost or heavy snowfall of memory

when my mother bundled us up
in our voluminous snowsuits

for the inclement weather.
since the forecast called for precipitation and
i was impenetrable to the elements outside

except for my eyes   memory in hindsight
is a stained pair of underwear held up

to the sunlight   now i see
beneath every zipped zipper, tucked mitten
clasped button, and tied earflap,

the difference between marching out of the house with some-
thing,
versus nothing.

Pull

The first time
I am called "nigger"
I am standing in my feet like clay

next to the security guard
of my summer sublet
the season I decide

to die rather than continue
to be pre-med. It is late
and this woman with two "bad" kids

is the only one awake
at 1 AM to listen
to my chirps of privilege

when a tall, muscular, drunk
Korean boy instructs the guard
to let him pass

without ID, room number or name

of the friend who lives upstairs.
She shakes her head with authority

when the boy forms a reaction
like a vowel—
pulls his hand from inside his jacket,

runs back towards the door,
pivots extending his forearms :
Fuck you fat niggaaaahhhhhhzz!

He wants to cock his finger into a gun
but it wriggles like a worm in mid flight
that must choose between the beak

or the drop.
I am 19 and know
I can survive a blow.

LAUREN MILICI

Alpha

let's pretend / be forgetful / blackout
when you touch me the first time / second time
wish I were dead / or elsewhere / can I hit you

as hard as I can? / kidding / we drink
to leaving / to Florida sinking / to the burnt down
buildings you left behind / we don't talk about the bruises

or your girlfriend / or why you came
through the window that night / I want
to tell her what it felt like

Purge

When the sun goes down, look for
his car across the street. Shut the
blinds. Lock the door twice. Picture him
pacing, or pulling at his hair. He doesn't
sleep. One night he threw a knife
at the wall. One night he wrote
your name in blood. She knows
too much. Do you? Think of the bar
he burnt down. Think of the car
he crashed & left. Think of
the pills, or needles. Tell
no one. Buy mace,
or a gun. Hide
under white sheets.
Forgive yourself,
maybe. Find him
in the back
of your throat.

STEPHEN FURLONG

The Game

I.

Trust comes together as family for a meal, a shared smile yet
eyes that focus on you, only. A hand brushes your hair back.
Hairs on your neck, though small, stand up at attention. These
hands nurture you, or so he told you, so he can sleep at night.
These hands reach dirty parts of you. They reach into your
head, above water yet, you are still drowning. Manipulation is
the hand reaching for your mouth—

II.

He calls you his "special friend," and he takes pride in making
you smile. The curve of your smile contorts upward like the
mountain in his pants. He tells you that the bigger it gets the
more you are winning. This game is to keep you at bay, in this
ocean, water, water, everywhere. In eternal limbo, you drown,
you struggle, you— (do not pass go)—the ice will always break
on your turn, falling further into the cold water of isolation—
You will be forced to return to these moments. You will be
forced to return. You will be forced.

III.

He watches you in the water, says there's something organic in
it. He asks you to shower, play; now his excitement has turned
into impatience. His eyes. They begin to shift again. He blames
you for getting him bothered, "You have become a bother."
Still his hand, over your body, a snake with venom, masks what
he calls love. His eyes change. You change out of your clothes.
He gives you options letting you believe you had some remote
control. There is no pause or fast forwarding.

IV.

Still, your head rewinds, replays, and it is always on high vol-
ume.

LILLIAN ANN SLUGOCKI

TRUE CRIME

1.

I've confirmed, through meteorological data, that it was raining in the early morning hours of March 16, 1970. A lawyer might look at this documentation and quibble with the taxonomy, and say, technically it was drizzling. But something was falling from the sky. It was a few degrees above freezing. Research also tells us the sun rose at 6:02 a.m. on Sunday morning. This confirms I'd been awake all night long because I watched the sky turn from black to deep violet, but fell asleep right before the sun rose. I believe the exact word, the perfect word, is pre-dawn. But I leave it to the court to parse this further.

2.

The bedroom set was blond wood with a headboard that had two compartments with sliding doors; one over my sister's head, one over mine. Sometimes we hid food in there. Parallel to the bed, on the south wall, a matching dresser with one tall horizontal mirror. The color scheme for the room was lavender. The coverlet was white with purple flowers, and it matched my sister's stuffed poodle, FiFi, who reclined on the pillows when the bed was made. The science of memory tells us that there are as many stories as there are people in the room. Each one is true. And while the arc of the narrative may vary a few degrees to the east or west, the geography of this room remains absolute.

3.

Blood, like ketchup, acts elastic. But dried blood has different properties altogether. Some of the viscosity remains, but it turns a dark rust color, and flakes easily off the skin. It also itches. By 5:40 a.m., as the sun was rising, and as the rain hit the bedroom windows, it was no longer fresh, like ketchup, red and thick, but oxidized on my skin, fused with the molecules of the epidermis. It had pooled inside the curved nail bed of all ten fingers, except the thumbs. It takes approximately five hours for this transformation. If we do the math, the blood was thick and red and elastic, at 10:40 p.m. This fits the timeline I have submitted to you for your review. Meteorologically, it hadn't started raining, and again the science will confirm this. I was in the kitchen being fed bacon, eggs, coffee and whiskey. Unfortunately, the only people who can confirm this are both dead. But blood evidence doesn't lie.

4.

The physical crime scene is located in the basement of this house. A search on Google maps reveals that much has changed in the neighborhood, since 1970—particularly, the property adjacent to it. In 1970, it was a wild tangle of trees, weeds, and a ramshackle wooden house. Despite the transformation of the adjacent property, the family home remains the same—
minus the large oak tree in the front, and the row of shrubbery below the living room window. It is still a one-story beige brick home with a curving sidewalk that leads to the front door, and a driveway that runs along the western side of the house. I don't know whom it belongs to now, but from 1962 to 2002 it belonged to us. The court is welcome to search property records to ascertain the accuracy of this statement. I may be off a year of

two on either end, but the location of the crime scene in 1970 in the basement, is indisputable. I'm sure it still functions as the laundry room, the ceiling foreshortened by the stairwell, next to the furnace.

5.

My birth certificate confirms that I came into the world on July 7, 1956 also in the early hours of the morning, about 30 miles south of the crime scene. I was thirteen almost fourteen on the night of March 15, 1970. I'd gotten my period one week after my 12th birthday. Statistically, this falls well within the range of normal development for midcentury girls. I learned to walk with a thick pad of cotton strapped between my legs. Kotex was the preferred brand. I worried about the smell, but was secretly thrilled by the thick, ketchup like blood. I wore a cotton training bra and my nipples itched. I can confirm that there were times that my body was out of control, and in fact, had a life of its own. I can also confirm that my body spoke a language that took a long time to learn.

6.

The concept of virginity is not so black and white. From a strictly linguistic point of view, it means a sense of wholeness, of being intact. Untouched. As in a virgin forest where the sun barely seeps down through a thick canopy of primeval trees. And no human has ever seen this light, this golden light. And no one ever will. From a sociological perspective, it's an important rite of passage for a girl. The popping of the cherry. Sometimes we bleed for that as well. But what happens if that child has never been untouched? For her, I would argue, the word is meaningless, through all its iterations. She will never be the princess who is rescued from the tower. In fact, that trope doesn't exist, and her body will never really belong to her.

In Summation:

On the night of March 15, 1970, I was thirteen almost fourteen. I'd had my period for a year and a half. It was raining and cold. I lived in a beige brick ranch where the trees of the adjacent property cast long shadows on the kitchen and basement windows. By the time it was 10:40 at night, it was over, and I was being fed bacon, eggs, coffee and whiskey. My bedroom was a perfect square, the color scheme was lavender, and my sister's stuffed poodle perfectly matched the coverlet and the pillows. Dried blood itches and is difficult to scrub from the interior of the nail bed. I don't remember entering the crime scene, but I do remember leaving it.

MAGGIE QUEENEY

Salvage

A winter spent sifting the second-hand hanging
racks of moth-gnawed wool, zippers
snarled along dress spines, unraveling hems
where thorns of old sweat prick, traces of blush

rose the collars. Balled receipts bloom
faded sums, smoke ghosts, and perfumes'
foreign tongues coil like hibernating snakes
inside purse linings. Tine scores scar

the faces of plates and time-tarnished links
of chain scribble a box's scarred velvet
insides—what draws me, sweat-enmeshed,
bolt-enshrouded, naked inside the infinite

other she's, to mock, try to disguise, to hide
the old hag following in her floor-length fur
like a mass grave held open and shining
a rayed aureole out of the wings of shot

silk lining to her bare, her milk-blue
skin scribbled maroon, pubic hair dull
as a pelt salted and taut, hanging
to cure over the headboard of a bed.

After-Assault Counting Out

That shirt. That night. I wore
that skirt, that dress, those tights.
Those heels I wore. I drank
those drinks: one, two, three—

My birthday, that night: thirty-three.
That morning, the first, I found
the bruise. I looked, that morning.
I found my shoes.

I found my shirt. That skirt found me.
I wore that night. That night wore me.
I looked, that night—drank one, two,
three: that shirt, that dress, those jeans,

those heels. I looked. I wore that
bruise that now wears me.

CHRISTOPHER MORGAN

The Shrimp Factory Haunting

from "Georgia Ghosts" by Nancy Roberts

the room
gathered
more shadows

a sound   rushing   heavy

a man
of   dark face
thrust   close to my own.

The shadows
around me seemed to grow

I   remember
it happened   quickly.

I gasped

he preferred
my hands   trembling.

the feeling   testing me
to reveal
to
someone

Extends His Hand

my father
who I haven't seen
in more than half my life
probably misses the hell
out of me
despite everything he's done
and recently I remembered
the time he flew here
to California
from hell-hole Georgia
—his first stab at "visitation"
with my sisters and me
—and my mom drove us all
to a McDonalds parking lot
to meet him
and it's evening-black
and we all refused
to go with him
of course
but in the very end
he reached his hand
through the car window

to me
and my sisters withdrew
in their seats
as my father extends his hand
and asks if I would at least
shake his good-bye
his little man
and his face is so sad
I'm somehow struck
by this overwhelming need
to forgive him:
this man, this hand
that slapped and punched
and shoved and pinned
and searched and fondled
and so much more
—all these ways
my family wouldn't know
for years and years
and years
but here I am
even after all he's done
with so much pity
and yes, even sadness
for this man
whose hands bruised and explored me
but still
my father extends his hand
and everything around it blurs
—my sisters, silent
my mother, eyeing me
and this hand
this only offer
of what he's done

this pause stretching
before my decision
and me refusing
refusing, refusing
—so yes, I'm still torn
knowing the reality
of this man
and his hands
and what they did
even if the heart hurts
so strangely

Doorway Sad Spell

1.
I remember trying to explain
to people over the years
how nothing was scarier
than an open doorway in the dark.
They never understood.

2.
Inside your room, everything can be
measured, observed, contained.
It's the doorway that threatens
additional factors. A feather,
a fist, a bit of cooling air, a roach,
a random bit of light, a sound
you can't quite understand.

3.
Which is to say, every doorway
is a potential breach.

4.
Or a sealable hatch. I remember

being chased up my stairs.
How I was always running
for the door to my room,
that point of transition,
to slam and lock in time.
I wasn't always fast enough.

5.
Whether by clocks, or charms,
or garlic, or fennel, or
animal blood, we bolster
our doorways against all
the outside world holds.
We reverse our hinges
when haunted, sprinkle
salt, and pray the spirits
will leave us be.

6.
I remember waking to my father
closing and locking my door
before all else that followed.
How I couldn't control
my own room. How
the doorway didn't just
block out the bad. Sometimes
it kept it all in.

7.
And after my family and I
moved across country
to get away, I still couldn't
tell my friends, or my
therapist, or my mother,

or my sisters what'd happened.
I kept inside my room, behind
its locked door, replaying the scenes
again and again and again and again,
burning the images into my mind,
trying to discover what I should have done.
But in the end it was just me, just
a boy and his monster behind a door,
and I couldn't let anyone in.

8.
Some people might forget,
but in the end, a door can only
delay. Only stall what wants
to come inside.

9.
Only in the last two years
have I started to fall
asleep most nights
without having my door locked.
I still get nervous when it's open.

10.
Some doors are stronger
than others. And some people
are stronger than doors.

GEULA
GEURTS

By The River

Men and women lay in the grass by the river, naked—
lapping up the sun like thirsty dogs.

I remember the cattails waving in the wind,
their long brown seed heads protruding from the reeds,

satiated by the open sun and abundant water.
They grow fast that way, faster than fertilized corn

in a field, faster than girls hitting puberty.
I was thirteen, the only girl there.

My white breasts—two little lumps, I wasn't sure why
my father brought me. I wasn't like the cattails

extending their white roots out into the surface
of the river, floating in the sun, exposed above deep water.

My legs were rooted in the stony bottom of the river,
water reaching my mouth. Lips soaked, I wondered—

how long can I stay this way before I turn blue?

Shabbat Meal

Just before dusk, you buttoned up
your white shirt, hovered

in the living room like a cloud
over the table cloth, the pots

lidded in silver, your mother's
candle sticks, until your eyes rested

on my blouse. You were
the incense & I the altar, enclosed

in your smoke. You took me
to a side room, pulled

at my skirt, took off
your skullcap to be closer

to God. When the sun went
under, I sat at the table dripping

semen, as your mother adjusted
her headscarf. My eyes hooked

on the challot, white cloth
covered, dew of shame. You said

a blessing over the wine,
but never looked into my eyes.

Good Whore

Rahav, Rahav,
let down your hair,
take us into your inner walls,
harlot of the city limits.

When he's done
he wipes me with a plastic bag:
there were no tissues.

I am a body of evidence,
alone on the bed.

Hide us in your night,
come lie with us in flax,
your flesh was made to save you.

I hear the toilet flush,
he puts his *tzitzit* back on—
the holy *shabbes* is approaching.

His mother expects him
home before dark.

Rahav could have refused
the men, but even a whore
is hungry for life.

Now he says he feels dirty—
we won't sin again.

He'll decide when I'm
ready to marry.

The good whore converts,
marries the righteous man.

In the meantime
my skin is red—

I am a body of evidence
alone on the bed.

Rahav, Rahav,
where is your scarlet thread?

SARAH
LILIUS

Boys, What Have You Done To Me

Tingles, brushes, electric stabs on my skin,
not spiders, tiny, with dark bodies.

It's you. It's collective you as memory
trying to find your way in.

Weapon on the shelf, in a drawer, under
the bed, dusty, ready.

My smallest mammal feel body
smell don't dance don't know

which way is out, my mind etched
with residue, the condensation

of yesterday, youth on a stick
swabs me, tests me, keeps me

just ripe enough, alert enough to know
dark places contain bones, threats.

Call me hen
looking for a haven,

No where safe to lay my eggs,
to let go entirely,

to nourish
another.

My Value As A Teenage Girl

I.

For awhile, I couldn't remember his name.
B meant nothing. The fog began,
chased me around the room.

B dressed dark, mismatched informal
like he didn't live in a nice house,
with a nice mother, little sister in pigtails.

One night he pulled me to his
lap with a gallon of milk, the label
faced away from my sight.

B drank. He put his mouth to mine.
I gagged. This began his dirty game.
He took me to his room.

I wore black, my harassment funeral
under way. I told myself
it could've been worse.

II.

L was quiet, creepy and strong.
The kind of boy who once killed small animals
because his mother was a mess.

I think he loved me, awkward, inkless.
One night on my family room
couch, everything secret went too far.

I screamed in disbelief, a fairy stepped on
magically violated, a twisted ankle
on a summer day, I wanted to slap him

because he laughed, because he thought
he owned my body, could enter it like
a public door smeared with fingerprints.

III.

The bulldozer of harassment
is rape. A is last, A is first.
I cannot recall the order of boys.

A brain scrambles the unreal, the horror
gnome with bloody knife, the unicorn
with bits of flesh around his horn.

I drove him home that night
with wet face and broken glass
between my legs, my car, a haven

of shame, the casket of normal
sexuality. I saw colors in the road,
the drizzle matched me.

He walked into school a fighting
cock who won the special meat.
A dumped me, a coin fallen

on the dirty high school floor.
There, trampled, I was a statistic
someone, somewhere, didn't record.

SHANNON
ELIZABETH
HARDWICK

How To Paddle With One Oar
In A Mental Hospital

The sound of breakdown is beautiful, a bare
sword in chest of deer
in the middle of nowhere, singular,

glinting as it enters bone

and earth. The sound of body-ballads,
whether a tree or a girl in a hospital room,
sixteen, barely able to break herself

open, yet, she's trying, testing

boundaries of breakage and who will be
witness—to her, the world's still
on the moment her pain became

real, just like that, one red

oar, the older man drifting

toward the child

pretending sleep, hoping
the body (protector) holds
the same answer for every thing.

From A Journal Of A 10 Year Old Girl,
Buried Under A Deer Blind

February 28, 1996

I just want a new pair of boots,
you know,
the pink kind, leather, tight
against my legs, so when I run
I can feel newness cut into me.
Dad didn't want to buy me boots.
Stared out the truck.

March 1, 1996

He can hear my thoughts. I rocked
up to my knees in the back of the truck
as weeds pushed through the muck. Alone,
we drove to the house. He can hear my thoughts.
I pushed my bangs back, bit my lip.

March 7, 1996

I know not to tell. His friends
laugh like coyotes when we
get home. With pink leather boots,
I could run faster,
down to the neighbor's
with the chickens and the girl with her
holes in the ground. We hide
things—notes, stones, pictures crumbled,
eyes scratched like her Barbies' by her brother.

March 10, 1996

A couple devil's claws from the mesquite
hugged my calves and I laughed, bleeding
down the alley back to dad. His friends,
the oil men, stood by the cooker telling jokes
until they weren't funny. They can hear
my thoughts. I ran for the screen door—

March 13, 1996

The neighbor girl's chickens, some of them
got caught in the wire, flapped, hung there,
silent, still, until her dad pulled them out,
one by one. You could hear the bones
go wild for second; his hands swept back
then let out a laugh, catching our eyes, quarter-
wide. The neighbor girl cried at the blood.
I didn't. I bit my lip harder.

The Big Bad Wolf First Thing In The Morning

You know what I love first thing in the morning? Seeing my childhood molester on the opposite side of the street as we wait for the crosswalk to change from hand to walking man. I can recognize his stance, his walk, his body from far, far away. He's older now with a sort of aging in his face as it drags from time and drug use.

I never thought I'd be in this situation again, but I moved back to my hometown in order to pay off graduate school debt after living in New York where I found a long-awaited sense of independence and power. But making a good income at such a young age, owning my own home, being a single mom in my home town—all of this has given me a different kind of strength and independence and I value both experiences. However, life has a propensity to move in circles and here I am, back to face my demons, so to speak.

The first time I saw him was actually five years after returning home. I started working with a client downtown and I assume he's a regular downtown, as well. I see him in jeans, always wearing a hat. Out here in west Texas, it is common for men to wear jeans to work every day. Although, unlike most men here who wear Lucchese boots and a fishing shirt or pressed collared shirt, he's opts for Polo shirts and boat shoes. He carries a brown leather briefcase and kind of bends down a little as he walks, as though whatever is in that briefcase is too heavy for him to hold comfortably.

It's funny how the body holds memory better than the mind. Often, we suppress these automatic reactions—the feeling in the pit of our stomach, the wave of anxiety, the tensing of muscles—when the mind can't comprehend the why, it shuts out the physical signals. Maybe we are crazy. Maybe something is physically wrong with us, etc. But as I've grown older, I've learned to listen to my body and honor its knowledge.

The first time I saw him, this past spring, something about his shape as he crossed the street in front of me made me think, *Why does he look familiar and why am I feeling anxiety right now?* My chest grew a bit heavy. As he passed me, I saw his eyes look up, briefly, at my face and then quickly look back down. Part of me wanted to follow him to the car-park elevator. Part of me wanted to face him again and see if he'd look at me like that again. I'm pretty sure I saw fear or shame or shock or surprise in his eyes. I turned around, watched his back as it walked away. I knew that guy.

As if the universe wanted to assure me I wasn't crazy, I happened to see him again the next day. I was able to look at him a little longer as he stood and waited for the light to turn.

I made myself look at him without averting my eyes. It's the kind of steady, studying stare that one makes in an attempt to challenge the other to do the same. Of course, he didn't. If he met my eyes, he quickly turned them away again. I saw his jeans, worn and soft as though he has two or three favorite pairs he rotates. I see the same hat, with the emblem from his favorite past-time. I see those damn boat shoes. I knew exactly who it was. I think my first reaction was a state of constant questioning: *Was this real? Could I trust how my body felt seeing him? Maybe I just want this man to be him and he's simply a representation?* But I hadn't thought about it in years. Why, on this random spring day, 21 years later, would the bodily feelings return? As a way of collecting evidence to return to in moments of wondering what it was that I actually saw, I snapped a picture of him as he walked past.

Two weeks later, I'm at my doctor's office to get my blood drawn as part of my yearly physical. There's a group of people there at 8 am waiting for their name to be called.

"Okay, everyone, I'm going to call you three at a time if you're here for a blood draw," said the nurse.

I'm scrolling through Facebook, not paying attention to the outside world, when I hear that last name called. The same last name of the man I kept seeing. After his name was called, I heard, "Hardwick." I didn't want to look up. My hands felt sweaty holding my phone. I put the phone in my purse, got up and, when I started walking toward the door, I saw his back. We proceeded like that in a line. I knew he heard my name. There are not many people in town with my last name and the ones that do are related to me. He knew my family pretty damn well. He knew me pretty damn well.

The nurse sat us down in a row of chairs. There was one chair separated from the other line, but facing it. I chose to sit there. He had on those leather boat shoes. Instead of jeans, he had on khaki shorts but still had the same hat from before. He crossed his legs. He buried his face in a People magazine. I'm sure he wasn't actually interested in whatever celebrity the magazine had on the cover. While he pretended to read, I continued to stare. When it became too much, I took a photo and texted the few people who knew anything about my past encounters with him as a child. I was looking for confirmation from a disinterested party that this was, in fact, the same man.

No matter how much I try to intellectually rationalize the situation, my body will always react in a certain way.

I try to focus on how old he looks. I think about how I could easily overpower him if I wanted. It's as though I'm looking at the Big Bad Wolf that terrified me in childhood and he's gone grey, lost his canine teeth and uses a walker. All growl, no bite. It's odd to see the Big Bad Wolf ready to hide away in the trees, whimpering, instead of bare his teeth and hunch down in preparation to pounce.

Part of me wants to say, *Come at me!*

It's no fun when the Big Bad Wolf is too weak to fight.

It's odd to feel sorrowful disgust for a defeated man.

This morning, I saw him again at the crosswalk, opposite me.

I still feel little-me inside, shaken. But as I walked past him this morning, mostly I felt in my own power.

Then there's the sadness I feel when I saw him—he must have so much pain in those bones, I think as he shuffles past me.

STEPHANIE
VALENTE

Wolf Girl

you run into an internet date six years later
& you are thinner & you are still pretty
he grabs the girl's ass but still looks at you
over whiskey sips, not quite placing
your face now with bangs + kohl liner
your face now heart-shaped
his face knowing + unknowing
i'm just a wolf-girl – my fur & pointed ears,
hiding.

No, Duct Tape Doesn't Actually Fix Everything

The end of our conversation was so final —
a drip in a coffee cup. As a teen girl, I said
enough rosaries to be holy, even though
I'm agnostic. I held enough sage & painted
lions to be a witch. When you ask if my arm
is my arm & I say yes & if you ask if my
body is still yours to trespass, I stutter.

ISOBEL
O'HARE

Above Average

she who is not ready   she has her own ways
takes pills   lies in her lover's bed
curled like a blade of grass she waits for the writhing wind
that aches and rocks her slender body   he whispers
against her neck untruths   the words that make her endure
the danger passes through her underground   she has
color in her face again   she lies on a clinic bed
while a cold probe enters her   hears that the state
of her uterus is above average   she is left
alone (again) with an image on a screen turned toward the wall
as if they thought she might not look
she was not always so big and so sure   you who fed
held her
took her photograph as she lay amongst the blades
tell her who she was   is   should be   she
moves from
room to room   bed to bed   page to page   she
wakes and rolls over
through the window the sudden stillness of trees   like a
film on pause

Blodeuwedd

the land is indifferent to her
no point in memorizing the rules
they shift like shafts of light across the mountains
every time she looks up
the game begins anew

some kind of heartbreak machinery

the jagged lines of the gorge disorient her vision
he guides her no more

this is a blue field   a
weeping ground

every flower
born from the rot of a woman

SHEVAUN
BRANNIGAN

Even Though We Were Vegetarian

At any moment we are no more than six feet from a spider.
One night, as you slept, I watched one
appear on the horizon of your neck,

like in a Western, the hero returning—
it climbed over the dune of your body,
up the steep face of your chin, and almost

lurched into your open mouth,
two of its legs waving in the air like
the horse being pulled back from the canyon.

I watched all this without waking you, I watched
the spider dip its leg onto your tongue
and decide to proceed forward.

Earlier that day we were at the fountain.
I stood with water around my ankles and stomped like
I was making wine, just to splash you. You said

I was being childish, I threw a nickel in the fountain
and said I wish you wouldn't call me names,
it counted five times over. That was the day

you told me you were only staying with me so
I wouldn't turn you into the police. "Before you," you said,
and I did, I mocked you in a whiny voice, because

I knew what was coming next. In unison we said,
"I was only afraid of mayonnaise."
It had become the punch line of our relationship,

begun at a party where I lurked underneath my
ex-boyfriend's arm, where my eyes further lurked
beneath thick bangs and makeup, scanning the room

and returning to you because you were laughing
at my shirt for power tools—I've Got Beaver Fever,
it said, while below, two beavers wielded chainsaws.

I liked a man with a sense of humor, which
I assumed explained your unibrow, your pants
tighter than tendons. You know this, and what followed:

your vomiting in the backyard, then coming up
to me with your hand over your mouth to ask for my number.
Days later, the courtship at the used bookstore

where you circled around me like a buzzard, until
you started pressing your body against mine,
brushing your mouth against my ear, unlike

any buzzard I've ever heard of—you started
whispering things filthier
than a D.H. Lawrence novel,

really hot stuff meant only for the bathtub.
We brought our bags of books to the car,
where you pawed at me like a breast-obsessed bear.

So I wasn't wearing makeup the day of the party.
So my bangs were up. It's my right
to change the story how I want to—just like how

after it happened I told you I had the right to call you
as many times at work as I wanted to in a day,
just to tell you to go to hell! and then hang up.

If I leave out the day I took all the Ritalin and the kitchen knife
and barricaded you from the apartment, it's for both our sakes.
After all, I may be crazy, but you were the one who proposed.

Next came the meeting of friends, the rushed merging of two
      lives
like hands interweaving to make a church and its steeple.
You impressed them with your guacamole recipe, but

everyone thought we were moving too fast, including us.
"We're not sleeping together," we would say,
 even though we were.

I've left out a six-foot-one problem, though, the ex-boyfriend.
I was still dating him on the side, which complicated things
when you and I moved in together. Even my hairdresser was
scandalized—

he called me his high maintenance client,
but maybe that was because of the bangs.
It was on his advice I decided to move out.

I can tell that I am moving too fast.
You were there. You know what happened.
I can slow down.

I can turn to the day
when everything shifted.
I had told you I was leaving.

I said we had to stop sleeping together.
I wanted to make things work with him.
You pretended it didn't bother you, just

that you wanted a proper goodbye.
We were both naked. We had been messing around.
You were on top of me

when you penetrated.
I said no.
You kept going.

You said, this isn't me doing this,
and then pulled out. Said,
that was me, the one who listened.

Penetrated again.
This isn't me doing this
became your chant.

Then things became frantic.
You said we should go to the police
because you had just assaulted me,

I comforted you because other men
had done it before and I was fine.
Then more, you called your mother

who told you that you had done nothing
wrong: rapists don't call their mothers
afterward, you called your ex-girlfriend,

the one who counseled assault survivors,
who said that this didn't
count. And you convinced me to stay.

Then talk of your grandmother's engagement ring,
and your mother and aunt took us shopping
for cheap, on trend furniture for our new life together.

I'd moved back in. I swear the apartment was now smaller,
we were always bumping into each other like
shopping carts at the grocery store. But I had my moments

alone. Like the weekend you were away for work, meaning
an intense two days of hotel sex, though it was
with one of your coworkers. I ordered movies

off of your pay-per-view account and let them play
in the other room on mute. And at night, when you slept so
    peacefully,
I paced through the rooms of our apartment and cried.

When I think of those nights, I think of the water tap
that never stopped leaking, no matter how many times
we talked about fixing it. That, and the shadows cast

by the window's security bars. Sometimes I stood so they framed
my face, hoping I looked beautifully sad to the women hooking outside,
staring back at me, thinking, now there's a girl with troubles.

Jackpot

I've become the type to buy lottery tickets.
Feel lucky just to have made it this far.
I don't have a set of numbers I play,
or a special coin for scratch-offs.
I use the fingers of this body
that has been hit by a car
then walked away,
had a man penetrate it as I slept,
then woke, and left without
the slit between its legs splitting
the body into two pieces,
labeled "before" and "after."
I let the machine generate
numbers for me because my life
is travelling to the clouds. So much
up in the air. My life
is the fallen balloons, too,
drifting deflated atop the sea,
the guarantee—like buying enough
tickets to win. I've come out ahead.

My kneecap is shifted,
my thighs hold the memory of his hands, but
these legs, they take me
where I want to go, to the sea, to the corner store.

DIANE
PAYNE

Difference Between Not Being Raped
Hitchhiking And Not Being Raped By Dad

Part One

After riding in a semi for a rather long time, the driver pulls out a gun and says, You know what I do to hippy hitchhikers?

You say nothing because it seems like a rhetorical question.

He sees a guy standing along this deserted Idaho highway, aims his gun, and says, I shoot them.

You say nothing.

But I'm not gonna shoot you. Oh, hell, maybe I will.

Of course he laughs.

You say nothing.

(This a familiar pattern that you recognize from when you know what was going on.)

We're gonna pull over and you're gonna get back there and you're gonna pay me for this ride.

He says this while driving, gun pointing at you.

But, he's not slowing down, so you figure this could be a bluff. He didn't shoot the guy on the road.

You are a bit of hippy(even though the hippies you admired but never knew because you were ten and living in Michigan, and they were 18 and living in California, the Flower Children hippie), so you pull out the Sucrets can from your pack (he doesn't even flinch, doesn't even suspect you may be pulling out a gun), pull out the crystals (right—navel gazing crystals—don't ask) hanging from a string, hold them in front of the driver and say: Would you like it if someone wanted to rape your mother? Your sister? Would you? Would you? Your voice rises a bit, not too much.

Who said anything about rape? I just said you owed me.

(See, it's never rape.)

He hands you a twenty, says you're looking skinny, go buy a meal. Before closing the door and driving away, he leans out the window, and says, No, I wouldn't like it if someone did that to my mother or sister and drives off, leaving you intact and twenty dollars richer.

Part Two

Dad drives a beer truck and Mom says, Go with your dad. Keep him company while he makes deliveries.

You say you'd rather stay home with her.

No, go. Then he won't get so drunk while he's driving.

You climb into the beer truck, which looks a lot like the milk trucks, and you sit on an empty beer crate because there's only a seat for the driver because they're not supposed to be hauling passengers around while they make their deliveries, and your dad rambles on about how he lived in the country growing up, and you already know this, so he turns up the radio and Johnny Cash, his favorite, starts singing about his prison blues, and you see the city disappear, and the farmhouses appear, then he stops at a bar out in the country, and tells you to come on in. I'm going to say you're my date. Don't say nothing and you'll be able to get a beer.

You're twelve and don't want to be your dad's date.

(For those of you who know this story, if you were retelling it your siblings, they'd say, Dad didn't deliver beer when you were twelve, you had to be eight. Or, the other sibling would say, You had to be fourteen! (exclamation mark = slut).

You got a truck filled with "free" beer, Dad ain't got no money, but you walk beside him to the bar, and the bartender says, Who's this pretty girl you got with you today?

Your dad chickens out because he figures the bartender knows you are his daughter, not his date, and he looks mad, and shoves you to the door. I told you not to say nothing.

After driving a few miles, he pulls up at an empty farmhouse and says, You can have a beer here. You don't need one in his damn bar. You don't want a beer, but he opens it. Then you know what's about to happen. Same shit. Over and Over. Don't you tell your mom or she'll die. You don't want her to die, do you?

I do this because you're my favorite. Doesn't this feel good? He doesn't wait for you to answer. He drinks so many beers you know your mom will be mad you let him get drunk.

I'll Flyaway Oh Lordy, I'll FlyAway. La la la.

Song goes on and on and on and on and just like that warm Pabst Blue Ribbon, and you know what else.

JENNIFER
MARITZA
MCCAULEY

My Black Girl

Girl you so strong, you so straight up strong.
Look at them chipless teeth, at them horsemuscle legs,
look at that fatless face, with no wrinkle nor tear.

Girl, you got them blueberry lips that never
flip down, that hair crinkled like dark mother, hey
queen girl, goddess lady, my girl girl girl

I'm proud to call you My Girl. Talkin' bout…
Hey, how you get that michelle-mouth, that bey-bounce,
that rosa-ride, that tubman-tough, hey now,
you ain't like them weak-willed light girls, yeah,
you near man-strong. Hey Man-Girl,
you My Man, My Man, My BlackMangirl, hey, hey!

damnit, girl, you stronger than some man. Ima call you
Not-Man, yeah, you so special you ain't no man nor girl.
You so highup Ima call you goddess, so holy you
invisible, you just a goddess with no color. Damn it girl,
you so special, you just floatin' like Lord. Oh, baby, you
so angel nobody knows where you flyin',
Look at you! Just lookin' like holy nothing.

Ima call you Nothing, you goddess girl.
Ima call you Nothing, hey, Nothing. So holy
nobody can see you.

Hey Nothing! you so strong bet I could sass you
and you'd say uh-uh or gimme that twitchy neck,
like them black chics in the movies do, 'cause they
don't need no man uh-huh. Hey Nothing,
bet I could throw any rock at your blackface,
bet I could stick any thick thing in you, bet you so strong
I could push you 'round and you wouldn't feel my hands,
bet you'd just say give it to me baby,
like them booty girls do on BET.

Hey, hey, bet I could make you take any lash and
red would never appear on that black
skin, nah, you wouldn't wilt for nothing.

Hey Nothing Girl, you thrill me. I know you could
survive anyone, 'cause you so damn
strong.

Ain't you?

Hey, my BlackNothingGirl
why you whining for awhile, nah
that's not what magicblackgirls do.

girl look into this cameraface and dance like you got
fever, gimme them bullet eyes like blackgirls in bad pain
do, camon, camon

angryassblackgirl, bestrongforme be strong
don't feel nothing, please, so I can

test my strength with your beast will.

heyhey
be how I like you best.

Not as you are, now, where I found you:
in a little room, dirty, lonely, and
vexed.

that just ain't no fun,
blackgirl.

(Previously appeared in *Luna Luna*)

40 Ways to Avoid Sexual Assault

1. Be alone, so you'll never have dangerous company.
2. Don't be alone, you need muscled protection.
3. Bring a man with you, women-friends attract suitors.
4. Don't bring any guy, just a boyfriend or male-pal.
5. Check: is your boyfriend angry?
6. Check: does your friend like you?

7. Don't look around, at anyone. Slap on sunglasses.
8. Don't put on sunglasses, men will want to fuck you.
9. Get very fat.
10. Don't get too fat, guys like fleshy girls.
11. Get thin. Be light-bodied so you can run fast.
12. Don't be too-thin, guys like twiggy legs.
13. Don't be tall either, you'll be easily seen.
14. Be leggy and long, you can spot the bad ones below you.
15. Be small and bird-like, you'll be quickly forgotten.
16. Don't be too little, someone might snatch you,
take you away.

17. Stay close to your uncles and fathers.
18. Check: Are your uncles and fathers kind?
19. Stay close to your mother.

20. Be careful of your mother, she might have a blind spot when it comes to you.
21. Don't go to parties.
22. Don't go to parties.
23. Don't drink.
24. Never drink.

25. Go shopping, that's where ladies act like ladies.
26. Don't go shopping, you might choose slutty clothes.
27. Go to school, you'll become an emasculating mate.
28. Don't go to school, that's where men groom you for love.

29. Avoid sidewalks, all the savages live there.
30. Drive everywhere you go, wherever that may be.
31. Don't drive anywhere, you might get followed.
32. Don't leave your house. Always be there, alone.
33. Never be in your house alone, someone will break in, steal everything.

34. Be ready.
35. Be innocent.
36. Be wise.

37. Find a large blanket. Make sure it is thick, wooly and wide.
38. Throw it on your body, the whole thing, nothing should be shown.
39. Hush, now. Disappear.
40. Repeat #39, until free.

(Previously appeared in *Public Pool*)

Nothing Ain't History

I am watching Cloverfield
Lane (the second one) which is a movie
about a girl who is deep-night
driving on Louisiana backroads
that sprawl and strain and disappear.
The girl is alone when John Goodman hits her car
with his rust-red pickup and she wakes alone
in John Goodman's sweaty bunker. He tells her
she should be grateful he has saved her, but
she is suddenly afraid of being alive.

While I watch the movie, I think about the week
before when I'd stopped at a Texaco for gas on
similar streets, somewhere on I-10, when
a Creole woman told me becarefulalonenowpretty
and she held my gaze long, and I told her yesyeahIwill
and Iloveithere but that last part soured in my mouth,
because Louisiana's swamprivers, white-sheet skies
and toffee women du Monde, throb with more history
and love than any chilly places I've lived before,
where nobody looked like me.

Still, I have never driven on roads so hidden
and bowel-black, so catacombed with American
past.

If you saw how dark those lampless streets could be,
you'd know how hard it is to only-love
highways that are flanked by long-pillared
plantations and Spanish moss hanging fat from live oak,
looking like elder beard, like shreds of slave clothes.
If you knew how chilling the voice of a whiteman
with a BlackRiflesMatter sticker can sound
when he sees you gassing your car alone, at a Texaco,
and says, hey beautifulwhereyougoinI'llfollowyouforsafety,
you'd know why that Cloverfield
girl was so scared.

I'll spoil the movie. The girl didn't get
killed by John Goodman. She did stay in the bunker
for a long time. You wonder if she'll ever find
a way out and she does. You think she is free,
but she has to fight these shadowy aliens
who thrash and claw at her from high sky
and prairie rookery. She beats all those aliens,
but the movie doesn't stop then.

Here is the ending:
There is no proper ending.
You don't see if the girl survives or not, you just know
she is somewhere driving and running,
driving and running,
until those Southern shadows catch up to her.

ALAINA
O'LEARY

Why I Changed My Name After I Was Raped

I've always wanted to change my name, but it wasn't until I was sexually assaulted in college that it became clear I needed to.

I remember one day I was on the phone with a customer service representative, cringing every time he said my name: Lisa.

Chafed, I was immediately compelled to go into my Facebook edit settings to change my first name. I did, and I pressed save. I couldn't wait to see how my new name looked: Alaina.
I loved it, but I felt I had to talk to my friends and family before I made such an important, permanent choice. I went into my edit settings to change my name back, but Facebook blocked my attempts: "You have changed your name recently. You may change it again in 60 days."

I've been an indecisive people-pleaser my entire life, but Facebook made the impossible decision for me: I was not asking for permission or opinions. I was simply changing my name. I did not consult my dad. I did not consult my girlfriend. I did not consult my best friend. In that instant, I became a new person. I was Alaina, the girl who was capable of making and defending difficult personal decisions.

I adopted the name "Alaina" from a friend I met when I was in seventh grade. I thought Alaina was the most beautiful name I'd ever heard. Almost as if it were meant to be, Alaina also had Irish origins (my family's background is Irish). It went beautifully with my middle name (Marie), passed down to me by my mom, whose first name is also Marie. Most importantly, when I asked my friends to call me Alaina, it felt like my name. It belonged to me. I didn't cringe when my girlfriend whispered it in my ear, or when my best friend called my name.

I never felt Lisa belonged to me. In a way, it never did. My parents were expecting a boy when they had me and were ready to name me Sean Patrick Leary—an overly Irish name if I've ever heard one. It wasn't until my mom was sitting in the hospital bed, holding me in her arms, that my grandfather started a last-ditch effort to find a feminine name. He stumbled upon "Lisa" (completely at random) and my parents made the life-altering decision within a few minutes.

This had an effect on me from a young age. I was about seven years old the first time I asked my parents to change my name. I wrote "Rachel" on almost all of my school papers and reports for the entire second grade. At seven, my mom was actually willing to allow me to legally change my name. It was my dad who requested that I wait until I was 18 to "think about it."

It wasn't until I was older that the name change became imperative. I was drugged and raped in a college dorm room, and my name became almost painful to hear. My assailant took my body, and thus, the right to my own personhood and identity. As I healed and learned to live as a survivor, I found it burned my ears to have my birth name associated with me, especially in intimate and sexual situations. I fought so hard against the idea that the person I was before the rape was a different person, but it was true. It was as if the old me had died and someone new had taken her place.

The most difficult roadblock to actually changing my name after experiencing this was my mom not being there. When I was 11 years old, my free-spirited, Elvis-singing, Stephen-King-reading mom passed away unexpectedly as the result of a seizure. I had her blessing from childhood to be the person I wanted, but I would never get the chance to ask her if she liked my new name. I could never ask her to call me Alaina Marie as we cuddled on the couch.

But when I finally changed my name on Facebook, within 10 minutes I was swamped with the comments, questions, and thoughts of other people about my new name. Friends were blindsided that I hadn't warned them. People were worried they wouldn't be able to stop calling me by a name I'd had for 21 years.

My dad, although he'd always been fine with my independence, was at first reluctant to call me by a new name. When I told him about my choice, he processed it slowly, and then said, "I don't know if I want to call you something else, but I don't mind that everyone else will." Fine, I thought, but a few days later, I was firm with him. I understood he'd been using the same name for 21 years and that I was his only child, but I didn't want any remnants of my name to remain.

I had to live every day with the memory of my rape, but I wanted to take control of my own identity as much as I was able to. I knew it would be like pulling teeth, prying the fragments of my old name from the memories of those around me, who for months would stumble as they said, "Li-Alaina," when addressing me. Facebook may have helped me make the decision, but I was the one who needed to be confident about it.

Few people made any real fuss about my name change, other than to ask in-depth questions about why I wanted to change it and how I came up with my new one. It was a revolutionary idea that I was asking every single person in my life to make a conscious effort to change their habits. It was a form of self-care and self-love that few had seen. Most of my family members and friends were proud and kind of awestruck that I was able to be so brave, especially since we live in a world where women who make their own choices are often called selfish. My aunt even gave me a handwritten card to tell me she was proud of my decision.

By changing my name, and asking everyone around me to change it, I was taking control of my life. My old name felt attached to what happened to me that night, to the person who used it without my permission, to the person I was before I was raped, and to a lifelong feeling that my name didn't fit me.

I took back my consent. I told people they weren't welcome in my life if they didn't adapt to my new name. I became Alaina.

ALEXIS GROULX

In the Beginning

my sister and I never shared
a mother — hardly the same father.
The only thing we could share
was space
on the same bed. Wasted time
talking about the photosynthesis
of plants.
We never compared bruises.

*

I was studying
dynamics of relationships
between constellations. She
spent time watching boys
from our streaked window.

Once she told me she believed
in aliens the way other people believe in God.
She was never one for science — not one
for fact.

*

Our father never showed an expression
other than fear.
Would get high, kiss his wife on the collarbone above
her right breast, then left. My sister always went
outside when he did. I couldn't stop watching them
thinking about the mating habits of birds. How some collapse
onto each other — how they often die because they can't let go
before they hit the ground.
It would have been nice
to see them crash — bloody on the sidewalk. Stepped
on by passerby without a thought.

*

Later, at a bar, I asked my sister if she had felt
the woman's body inside of her. I could tell
from her growing pupils she never had. A deer just hit
by a speeding truck, pupils struck wide when life leaves them.
My drink still had frost on the rim
when I left her at the table. I haven't seen
her since.

PATTY
PAINE

Marked
for my sister

on the playground

                    wrong touch they call it

children in coats

                    become a scent

the color of pigeons.

                    picked up again and again

tiny lungs

                    it might be your stepfather's

swell inside chests before

                    drunken lunges, thick-tongued

shrieks peal out

threat. *Don't tell. Don't tell.*

into crisp morning air.

        or your best friend's brother lures

a girl twirls

        you into the woods

into a blur of red

        then another tickles

cheeks and yellow hair.

        as cover for thrusting

another urges

        cold hands into your panties

a swing higher and higher.

        you'll spend years believing

I long to hold her

        it all must be

above the earth

your fault. But, please. Listen

to keep her

carefully. It's not.

suspended in air.

It's not.

ABIGAIL
WELHOUSE

Gone

Gone, they say. *She brought it on herself,* they say. She told him
maybe, if she didn't have a fluid-bound boy back home. Was it
blood or wine or water. Was it ocean or semen or spit.

I am always being told to calm down. I am always being told
to calm down by men. I am always being told things, but these
things are not truer than what I say back.

I wish I could say
I left when I found out—
but no, not yet.

Sailing Lessons

Mary flirts with sailors.
A dragonfly lands on her navel's jewel.
She reclines with a glass of Riesling.

The sailor describes knots.
Mary thinks of Joseph. The carpenter shop. The veins in his
arms.
Another sailor asks Mary to sit on his lap.

Back at the apartment, the three of them kiss,
loud through neighbors' walls.

> *(I don't miss Joseph——*
> *I miss feeling human.)*

Her body hits the wall.

In the morning, there are bruises:
where hip hit wall;
where tongue met throat.
It hurts to speak.

Just as well,
since she will never find the moment
to mention it.

JACKLYN
JANEKSELA

Coping

Coping looks like panties in a plastic bag, tucked deep in the laundry basket, saved as proof.

Coping is pouring out a handful of your boyfriend's Percocet while drunk, then throwing some back into the bottle because you don't really want to kill yourself.

Coping is throwing up on a pen he's shoving down your throat.

Coping looks like a dead face, it's an ugly face that stares back from all mirrors, reflections, and dreams; it's a dead face that your ex, who just got outta jail, holds in his hands.

Coping looks like moving everything from one side of a studio apartment to the other because change.

Coping is paying a psychologist to criticize why you didn't ask her about the scratch on her face –a cat; and somehow making the rape about your father –typical.

Coping is unfriending him but still looking at his profile picture.

Coping is not eating peanut butter for years because that's the last thing the perpetrator ate in your apartment.

Coping looks like dying your hair black and getting as close to death as possible, but not crossing the line.

Coping is getting back into Marilyn Mason and writing shit poetry.

Coping is digging underneath a fingernail rather than cutting.

Coping is drinking into stupor after stupor, falling down a flight of stairs like a ragdoll and getting a hairline fracture on your collarbone.

Coping is drinking into another stupor where you throw chips at the party hosts.
Coping is drinking into yet another stupor and thinking your desk chair is the toilet; you piss right there while your boyfriend stares, horrified, from the bed.

+   +   +

You never think it will happen to you, the old cliché. And it was very much like that with me. It didn't happen during my childhood, adolescent, pre or post graduate years. That means I was free, I had escaped; I was immune. I thought I was too something or other for it to happen to me, whatever that something was built a straw house around my body.

Those wolves come in sheep's clothing, that's no lie. Almost all rapes are at the hands of someone you know. That's also not a lie, it's a true truth, it's a real as it gets.

I had also thought that I would die without breaking a bone. As if my bones were somehow impenetrable to damage or hurt; I thought the same way about my body, my vagina. I said, I'll go to my grave with all my bones solid, without a single one broken; and I was sure as fuck about it. Yet, I broke a bone. And I'm still coping with it. I cope as I push myself through yoga poses that put pressure on the bone. Sometimes I make it through the end of the pose, sometimes, I don't; but all the while I try, that's me pretending that the break never happened. That click I hear when pulling up my panties or putting on a jacket, that's not from a broken bone, my bone somehow got outta place. That is not coping, that's denial.

I did that, too. I did it on the morning after it happened.

My mind was coping, it said it wasn't him. It said the sound of him violating you wasn't what woke you up, you made that shit up because you're sick and twisted, it's all in your head. It said you didn't feel him touch your vagina, that was a mistake. It said the sound of you slamming the door after he left was just a bad dream. It said you were drunk, bitch. It said you flirt too much, slut. It said you let people get too close too quickly, loser.

My brain said lots of things, but in the end I had to accept it and walk away from it without naming it. Like I did once in college when I think I might have been raped but wasn't sure, so I just collected my clothes from the floor, got dressed, and went back to my dorm room; the irony is the following weekend I watched *Kids* for the first time. Like the time, years later when, in a dirty hotel room, I teetered between a blackout state and a haze as I sloppily tried to push a man away who was pushing himself into me from behind.

I didn't say his name at first when I told my boyfriend, friends, and co-workers. Everyone knew him.

When I named him, I faced myself, I made myself fearless for the times I wasn't. I looked at what had happened as something that happened to me, not something I provoked, not something I asked for, not my fault. I named him because it was him. It wasn't anyone else and it surely wasn't me. I named him because I wasn't brave enough to name the others; however, the last one doesn't have a name. He remains an unknown, a face that won't fade into the darkness where I sometimes rest and force myself to cry.

Once it happened, other women's stories seemed to come out of nowhere. There wasn't a woman who hadn't been a victim. Now if that doesn't depress the fuck out of you. I wonder about whether I want to be a mother to a little girl, to bring her into this world where she's surely to be violated, too. That rape is more likely a part of her future than not is fucked up.

Then it seems that it would only be a matter of time until I met my own fate, a fate that had already touched me because it touched all female, yet it remained unclaimed; a circle within a circle, a story within a story, a rape within a rape. Some might call it postmodern. I call it death. Ever since I had begun to pursue boys and vice versa, I've died a little each time. Even today as I write this while my husband washes dishes, I realize I move farther and farther from love and with each passing relationship I'm less likely to love and less affected by it. Cold and distant, I am a snowflake that never melts. I float just above your head and only wish I could cry. But crying is for humans and I've long since made love to death and let him suck the meat from my bones; bone and blood dry.

I'm as dead as anything else. I cope by calling myself death and saying I can no longer love. I cope by denying love and cringing at the thought of being a mother. I cope by destroying every relationship I've ever had and will continue to do so. I cope by being alone. I cope by being alone in the midst of a relationship. No one can get close to me, the illusion is that you think you're close to her, but it's all part of her magic. Her smile is no smile, look at her eyes. Her kindness only means she's scared you'll hurt her. Her rage is the clothing she wears daily. She copes by coiling inside herself and instead of considering a daughter becomes her own daughter and births herself again so she can start over, so she can forget, so she can cope. So she doesn't have to be me.

ERIN
MCDONALD

The Smallest Harm

He asked if he would see me at the club later. Those are the last words I ever heard from my rapist. I hear it in his voice, just as I hear his voice commenting on my pubic hair. I don't remember any of our other conversations. It is silent. Silence is as much a noise as any other, it is an emptiness that is heavier than anything comparable. I do not remember his face yet I recall the images behind his face. I remember the face of his friend, the colored lights in Coco Banana (a club later shut down). I recall how the eggplant I bought from the street cart had tasted. I remember how him slapping my ass on the street at two am felt, how it made me feel, how his fingers felt, bruised. I remember a lot of things yet I cannot recall his face. In a strange way, him raping me in the morning was the smallest harm he did to me. In a strange way, in a small way.

It was not the first time I felt small, it was not the last time I would feel small either. Some people are so accustomed to becoming tiny when necessary that they are no longer surprised when people take advantage of it. I was in denial. I was that person who had to have four people confirm what had actually happened for me to accept it. I have always been the person who would take care of others, I had grown up in a house built around another person's victimhood. I had watched the house be built, set on fire, ashes, built again. I had watched this process over and over again, all the while standing inside of it. Maybe that is why it was so surprising that it had happened to me. I had seen myself as a separate unreal entity, invincible. In an odd sense, I had believed I had learnt better by watching, instead of being cautious, I believed myself protected from the experiences of those around me. As if, because I had left that house, that I could no longer be burned. You never really leave the house, you are just at different stages of the fire.

It had been burning for a while by that point, I had been burning. A soft burn at first, a day spent too long in the light without sunscreen. My skin was pink and peeling. My rape found me on my hypothetical blanket, poured gasoline on me, and lit a cigarette. At first, I thought I was okay. I went to class, continued going out to the club with friends, and I fucked. Fucking was my one reprieve from my thoughts, which at that point had succumbed slowly to the fire. They had picked a room in the house, painted it blue, locked the door, lit a few candles in a room already becoming ash. Fucking allowed me to be silent, to be voided, to not exist. My body was only a vessel for an orgasm, a momentary lapse in thought. I fucked a businessman from Mumbai, a musician who later appeared in *Rolling Stone*, and I even fucked a boy who tried to love me even though he didn't understand the importance of knowing my favorite color. I fucked until the white hospital like dorm room walls no longer reminded me of waking up to the fire. I fucked until I forgot that my rapist had slept on my mattress. I fucked until I didn't recognize my own voice unless it was moaning. Fucking wasn't the only thing that was an escape, like most trouble it came with a pair.

There was a bar in Hangzhou that served cocktails with bendy straws. I would often go there, drink as many cocktails as my body could handle (which turned out to be many) and smoke hashish with my friends. There was one night where a Pakistani fashion designer, with his strange posse of men in their forties, drove us around to various clubs. They had picked one man to be sober, as he drove around a bunch of drunk American and European girls, buying us all drinks at any club we went to. Life was odd then, the fire was burning but I could keep it sectioned off as long as I had a drink in my hand and a story for later. I never kept track of how much I would drink, mainly because then I would probably have to admit I had a problem. I was nineteen. I was beautiful. I was destructive. I felt like a warning sign walking: Do Not Touch Me, I Only Know How To Burn.

You can only keep a fire sectioned for so long though, at least the appearance of it. Before I knew it, everything was burning and in turn I burned everything. The morning of September 5th, the strange blur of bodies, was the smallest harm. The burning that came after, that led to so many people viewing me as a burden and abandoning me in the Hangzhou smog was the greatest. I will never forget being told by my best friend that I was the biggest anxiety in her life. No amount of trauma therapy will fill the empty those words left in me. I built my new house in the ashes of those words. They still sting me daily. I am trying to not blame her. I am trying to remain tender. I am trying to not let September 5th and the burning define me but I still see his empty faceless figure when I am sobbing in the shower. I still am hit with the realization that I will forever always be this heavy and this small. Many plants grow and are rejuvenated through ash, stronger and radiant. Even the smallest and most vulnerable plants give forth the most edible fruit, despite the burning, they grow. I can no longer be a house on fire, hoping that something will douse out my flame. I must be a forest flourishing.

SLOANE ELIOT
MARIEM

to you alone.

what heaven is there for girls like me who love death like an ab-
sentee father,
who want to be filled with its emptiness,
who need the sticky cream of its void
to birth black holes inside them

he appeared to me again in a dream
unexpected in an afternoon respite after a long absence and
sat quietly at the end of a table while my face reddened and
peeled, rash-like
and i missed him, worshipped his eyes like flies, like beelzebub,
silently kissing his plague-ridden feet in my mind

when i forget to maintain my anger, i feel your danger creep in
again and again with the memory of your soft hands and foreskin
has there ever been a greater love than your fists on my face,
drawing blood and desecrating the vessels within me

you strike the air around my body and your want to hurt shifts
palpable;
i feel electric, magnetic, our current flows from god itself.

i can't breathe without you and must learn to be dead but
i'll never walk that golden staircase to transcendence
because i don't get hot for what's right

what plague is this that holds me down in willing participance
to your violation
my misery stays hungry for your hate and
i relish the vitriol you spill in my face

i live inside your wailing.

i'll lie still again beneath you to feel your head slip to its home,
to feel your hips angle toward god
 and push my insides toward sweet oblivion

i'm out of body and see myself in black and white,
bathed in red light inside your domain where you keep me and
it's home
from here, i watch myself arch my back to breaking's point,
freeze time to preserve a moment's agony in memory,
a beauty, a tribute to this black beast i serve who re-appears on
whims to tear me down

and if i could just trust in your devotion to destroying
me and only me, i might let you finish the job

i want to open my veins and spill my red disease to you alone

second person.

you think about writing a poem in second person.
you wonder if it will help him understand.
you know it's a little overdone
but he's never even heard of lorrie moore.
you feel doomed.

it's a monday evening and you're on the bed, but the pillows
aren't;
they're on the floor where you've thrown them. you can't
breathe.

you can't breathe and feel doomed.
you are alone and drowning.
someone walks on the beach, sees you, keeps walking.
everyone keeps walking. you are drowning. you feel doomed. you
are alone.

you are currently having an emotional breakdown.

you are crouched in a fetal position with your forehead pressed
into the mattress.
you are sucking in huge ugly gasps of air, can't hold on to them.

they keep walking. you are alone.
you're gasping. the pills are not enough. you can't breathe.
you imagine you have gills, are drowning on land.
he's smoking a cigarette on the windowsill.

he says, "do you want me to leave."
he takes a drag of the cigarette, crosses his legs.
you have no voice; suck deep ragged breaths. can't breathe.
your gills flex uselessly.
you want anything other than to be alone. the pills are not
enough.
he leaves you like that, crouched and gasping for air.
you are alone and drowning.

you wail into the mattress for twenty minutes until your voice
runs raw.
your gills flex uselessly. you feel doomed. you are drowning.

your eyes are swollen, nearly shut.
you don't recognize yourself in the mirror anymore.
your lips are dry and cracking but you can't care.
you are not okay. you are drowning, doomed and alone.
the pills are not enough.
your gills flex uselessly. you can't breathe.
tomorrow you'll taste blood where they split.

catch your breath and call him.
he's turned off his phone. straight to voicemail.
you're drowning and doomed;
the pills are not enough. you are alone.
you can't breathe. you will die like this.

you text several people. you feel doomed.
your head is pounding. your eyes are pounding.

everything in you is throbbing an ugly throb.
you are drowning, useless gills flexing, lips dry and cracking.
you will die like this.

you are alone. the pills are not enough.
your lips are puffed and chafed. they crack. the salt from your
tears gets in them.
you don't know what to say other than i need help.
you type, i need help.
people walk by on the sand.

minutes pass. you can't breathe. he comes back.
you're gasping. you need help.
your face doesn't feel like your face anymore.
it's been replaced with the piggish mask of desperate grief.
the grief can see your certain death.
it whispers the details in your ear.
you feel doomed. you are drowning.
your gills flex, useless. you will die like this.

he lies in your bed and touches between your thighs. you feel
doomed.
you are alone and drowning.
you will die like this, gills flapping, touched between the thighs.

your phone makes a sound. he asks who. demands.
you say you needed help, that he wasn't there. you did. you do.
you need help. you are drowning and alone. your gills flex.
the pills aren't enough. you feel doomed. you will die like this.

you twist away from his hand between your thighs.
you think, help. you wait for him to realize.
your eyes are swollen shut, gills flapping.
you wait for him to realize.

he must know you're drowning. you can't breathe.
he must know you will die like this.
you feel doomed and alone.
you think, help.

he says, "if you won't fuck me I'll go to someone who will."
you are doomed and drowning, alone. gills flex, useless.
you can't breathe. you will die like this.

you sigh, your breath trembles, wants to escape you.
everything wants to leave you alone.
everything walks away. you will die like this.
you are alone and drowning. you need help.

you feel doomed. you have to remove your tampon.
he says, "do it here." you do it there.
you lie in bed again. stare at the ceiling.
stare at nothing. say nothing. stare. gills flex.
he says, "take off your pants." you take off your pants.
he sees you're still wearing underwear,
says, "christ, do i have to tell you how to do everything?"
you take off your underwear.

you're still wearing your sweatshirt and the ugly piggish mask.
you put your head on his shoulder. you need help.
he says, "fuck this," moves to leave.
you feel doomed. you are alone. you can't breathe.
the pills are not enough. you wait for him to realize. you're
drowning.

you put your hand on his cock and he moans. you will die
    like this.
you think, help. you don't look at him, don't say anything.
stare at the ceiling. stare at nothing. you feel doomed.

you just move your hand and he moans.
say nothing. keep moving your hand the way he likes it. you
can't breathe.

he climbs on top of you.
you, in your sweatshirt and pig mask of grief.
you say nothing. you don't move. you look anywhere but his
face.
stare at nothing. stare at the ceiling.
you wait for him to stop. you wait for him to realize. you need
help. you're drowning.

he fucks you. you stare at the ceiling, say nothing. help.
you wait for him to realize.
he walks along the sand, sees you, keeps walking.

you can't breathe. you're drowning. your gills flex and flap
uselessly. you need help. the pills are not enough. you stare at
nothing. you are doomed. you wait for him to realize. you will
die like this. he comes.

AMY JO
TRIER-WALKER

Especially If Legs Have Atrophied

It's usually uncomfortable during a heart attack.   I gave up
It's a vise being tightened.   without seeing it

Many experience vague   took too much energy
or even silent
symptoms they miss.   when I had to pay attention

                                                                   I had to
Women tend to have hurt   sense
not only in their main arteries,
but also in the smaller bruises   where his keys were
that supply blood to the retinas.   if the water was hot enough

Patients often complain of a tiredness   when he wanted laid
in between the ribs. They say
they can't.

                                                  when he wanted a bowl
                                                  when he needed whisky

Sliced leg can be gradual or sudden, and it may wax
and wane before he comes.
If you're asleep, you will faint to go back.
    if he was about to hit my dog

                              if he wanted his guys over
Breaking out in a nervous, cold sweat is common.
if they said something he didn't like
                         or talked to me

           if we could ever afford food
             that didn't make me sick

Sometimes women mistake
stomach pain that signals home
with heartburn, the flu, or a stomach ulcer.

                   when I should move furniture
            to cover the holes

Other times, women experience severe abdominal pressure
that is glass through skin.
               makeup
It may confuse women who expect their pain
to be focused   does not work
and crushing the chest.   as well as a
bookcase

Women generally wait longer   I had to pay attention
before emergency room.   for when I should thank him
again
There are dishes.   saving me from pills and
starving

                    from the first rapist boyfriend
            he always said he should have killed
                                when he had the
chance

It may feel like squeezing or fullness,   saving me
    from being alone

and pain can be anywhere   I had to sense
in the cervix, not just on the left side of the bed.
    when not to hide

                                when I had to say, yes
If having trouble breathing   it's alright you fucked her
                    when I walked in

for no apparent reason, you could
check your throat.

                    yes, you should study philosophy
                        politics   production

        yes, I know I've gained too much
                for anyone else   to stand to look at me

yes, I'll clean up your shit
and puke

yes, of course you're right. I don't know
what I was thinking.

yes, it turns me on
when you choke me

Chest pain is most commonly a symptom   yes,
of controlled,   we'll manage
but some women   without your job
experience it differently.   again

yes, I'll go
to the clinic
I'll take care
of it

yes,
I love you
yes, I know you need me
too much   to kill me

Some women who have hearts feel
extremely tired, even if they've been sitting still
and especially if legs have atrophied.

        yes, I'll try
    to speak   louder
                takes a lot
          of energy

MARTY
CAIN

Kids Of The Black Hole, Part II

In college, my friend was drunk and threatening to hurt himself. He'd done it before. He'd hatch-marked his arms and shown me his scars. He'd said, *Look what you made me do.*

This night, I didn't want him to be alone. I told him to spend the night in my room (on the floor). He lied down. He knocked over my lamp. I knew he'd had feelings for me. He'd told me so. We'd kissed before. He'd asked me to blow him. I'd said no. I turned off the light. I don't think I spoke.

He said, *Are you really going to make me sleep on the floor?*

When I experience trauma, the first thing I do is aestheticize it. When I make art, the first thing I do is traumatize myself.

I'd shown my friend the manuscript for my first book, *Kids of the Black Hole*. It's directed towards an addressee who is, more or less, a version of my friend. He said, *This feels like the narrative of someone who was raped.*

It feels good and it hurts.
It feels good and it hurts.

I felt bad. I said, *Get in the bed.* It was a twin. He was right next to me. He may have been crying. I can't remember what happened next. I remember he pressed himself on top of me. I remember he said *Hold me* and grabbed my face and tried to kiss me. He smelled like whiskey. This is not accusatory. There was no genital contact. I remember he was on top of me longer than I wanted. My head was empty. I dreamed of a dentist scratching my teeth with metal. It was meditative. Black light, blue light. I don't know what happened next, but I know I pushed him out of the bed, or, I got out of the bed; I told him to leave the room, or, I left the room. Then I don't remember.

I was an object of desire: he made me an object.

In graduate school (two nights ago), I remembered this happening. I remembered this happening because I saw a rape scene in a mediocre horror movie and it shook me; it shook me and I spent most of the night drinking whiskey and smoking cigarettes and reliving the past and staring into the radiator feeling sick. The wound of historiography.

The next day I cleaned the house and called friends on the phone and Jesus Christ it was fucking clean and nothing about it was human. A false before; the past as a shattered mirror that breaks me apart when I see my face.

This is still my confessional poem.

I don't know if it's real.

You are welcome to leave it.

It is 11:49 am on October 17, 2016, a Monday, and I should be doing work. I should be reading psychoanalytic theory. I'm scared to be writing this. It's common to not recognize patterns of abuse—to acknowledge them as abuse—until much, much after the fact.

Even after you've aestheticized them.
Even after you've made them into a poem.
Even after you open the wound that made you an object.
Even after you let it sing you into a subject.

I don't know if I'm uncovering wounds, or if I'm making new ones; I don't know which is worse. There is nothing "good" about this prose.

On a certain level, I believe it's my fault.

The wound is not real.

This, too, is perhaps a common sentiment for victims of abuse.

STEPHANIE
BERGER

The Past Is Not The Past

In the swirling morning airport, I discovered your
smile quite eerily at the bottom of my cappuccino,

in every grain of the pistachio flour in my cardamom-
scented muffin, and in the mirror of the airport

bathroom, tiny holocausts in her eyes.
Yesterday I wrote the song that I will sing

tomorrow, fat as a lady with a piano
in her pants. Yesterday I blew the glass

through which I will blow smoke tomorrow.
Smoke signals, far reaching, universal, so

superior to language. How do I separate
this feeling in my lungs from the one

in my heart? Breath shortens as the beat
quickens and the heart in pain is sentient

suddenly in every part of her body—
lungs, gut, throat, mouth, and finger

tips, in the lobes of each
of her ears, a conscious heart.

Yesterday, beneath a rock, I discovered the key
to a door that I will build tomorrow—in order to leave.

Do you hear that? The truth just sounds different.
Considering one's future adds a certain dimension.

We lived for a while in a dirty love nest
constructed of feathers and fallen branches.

I returned years later and the furniture was expensive
beautifully beveled, carefully crafted, curated, and I knew

dysfunction was our natural state. I could see myself in the
baking
pans. I held one up to my face as I left and left

a small streak. No longer could she rest
on the laurels of her dumbness.
Learning, at first, does feel like a loss.
Occasionally she would let go by

some misogynistic half-baked truth
launched from the mercurial knee-jerk of the patriarchy.

Later, she wrote a terrible Yelp review
for our habitat in general. Consumed for hours,

literally feasted upon, by her imagination.
Spirit mouths caressing her body ominously.

Violated even in her dreams, even in his.
I detest this disjointed dream.

It's a disease you have to battle like a knight.
The sky is sick, but it doesn't groan.

The neck of the tree is stiff and cracks
but it never moans. A branch

falls. A kind of necessary surgery.
Even the weight of the page

is lighter without an appendix. Superfluous,
those endless inky letters in the back of the book.

Even the moon grinds its teeth at night.
And the man in the tree. And the woman

in the clamshell. She grinds those pearly
whites to form a fine powder

that she smooths onto her face in the morning
after a night of overindulgence in the sea.

I live inside a hideous shroud, wrapped around
my shoulders like an old carpet. Weighty

as the past. Heavier than any contemporary
object. Clearly she is an easy lay because of the lightness

of her outerwear. Mine is heavy but with holes, exposing
a little underwear. Hate me because I'm beautiful,

not for the extra bit of bravado I've projected around
this note. At night even the piano grinds its teeth.

Now all of the time we spent together
will get lost to more time. Like a dog

who bites down chasing its own tail,
or an angsty teenager or any kind of artist,

time consumes itself, destroys itself, bleeds
into the coffee we consume to get it back.

Even the earth shakes in fear that it will break.
And the sky cries hard for a little while

like an overtired child. I've got to get this down
to get you back. Tall and hairy with a massive

cock like an 80's porn star and the saddest
eyes I've ever seen, his mind searching as the sun.

In a chariot, quick to snap the reins and stain
the stars in blood. English is a language of water

and wonderful for washing clean the nuances
of a disaster. I watched you like a screen

as we drove across the seas. Time passed and
my subconscious browsed for subject matter.

Every morning we stirred around the same
time, bodies entangled like warm wires. I watched

you wrap a cord up to be orderly. I watched you
like a damn soufflé that never rose.

CHRISTINE
STODDARD

A Night in San Juan

When I think of San Juan, Puerto Rico, I think of the Santa María Magdalena de Pazzis Cemetery nestled by the bay. That's because my first visit to the city was not a festive tropical affair. Lost in reflection, I gazed out at the white tombstones and statuary huddled by the seawall. It was a beautiful sight, but not exactly the defining image for most people's Puerto Rican vacations. Of course, the circumstances surrounding my trip were less than typical.

My childhood best friend won a three-day vacation to San Juan in a sweepstakes, but couldn't go because she was starting medical school. When she offered the prize to me, I immediately accepted. I turned in my final assignments for my summer classes and hopped on a buss from Richmond to New York. Once in Manhattan, my parents picked me up at the station and whisked me off to JFK. My parents were happy to do me the favor on their way to Connecticut. Besides, this way they could see me off before my trip. Unsurprisingly, there were far more flights to the island coming out of the Big Apple than my native nation's capital area.

I don't remember the drive from Manhattan to Queens. What I do remember was sitting in my parents' car for a few quiet moments after I had already said good-bye. My mother stopped me with "Wait," but she didn't continue. Her look of utter trepidation made me wonder if she could bring herself to talk.

"What's the matter?" I finally asked.

"Don't get into any taxis by yourself," she said.

I scoffed at her overprotectiveness, but swiftly regretted it when she added, "My mother was raped by a taxi driver."

My annoyance suddenly dissipated. I was 22 and had never heard this before. What came next explained why.

"When I was 14, my mother took a taxi alone and the driver pulled over to the side of the road and raped her," she went on. "He dumped her in the ditch and left her for dead. When she regained her strength, she walked the rest of the way home. I was in the kitchen when I saw her clothes all torn up. She had terror in her eyes. I knew something horrible had happened."

My mother shook as she told the story. All these years later, she still felt so much rage and sadness.

My mother rarely talks about growing up in El Salvador when the country was on the cusp of a bloody civil war that began when she was in her teens. She left for good when she was in her mid-twenties and moved to Miami to marry my father, an American journalist who had covered many Latin American conflicts. When she does mention those times, her stories are often brief but horrific. The tale of my grandmother's rape was no exception.

By this point, the cars behind us were honking, so I didn't have much time to react other than to say I was sorry and that I promised to be careful. I leaned forward to squeeze my mother's quivering hand and then hopped out to catch my flight.

I was in a dreamlike state until I arrived in San Juan. Suddenly hyper-vigilant, I boarded a city bus at the airport to get to my hotel. I observed everyone on the bus and kept track of their movements, only looking outside to note my surroundings.

When I got to the hotel, I learned there was no room service, so I asked the clerk where to eat. He admitted the area was sort of a dead zone, but there was a Burger King a few sketchy blocks away. I was too hungry to consider options further afloat and set off into the night.

I think every woman has a natural fear of walking someone alone at night. Even if we're strong, even if we're fast, even if we've taken self-defense classes, we know that we are vulnerable to men who want to do us harm. Our male attacker will almost certainly be stronger than us. What hope is there for us once we've been overpowered? My mother's story had doubled my normal level of fear. I must've jumped two feet when a driver catcalled me and hyperventilated the rest of the way to Burger King. I placed my order, gulped down my sandwich, and then raced back to the hotel. Once I locked myself in my room, I felt all of my muscles relax and fell asleep from pure exhaustion.

Over the next couple days, I drifted from historical site to site, overwhelmed by a sense of helplessness. Usually, I enjoyed traveling alone because it allowed me to see exactly what I wanted at my own pace. Yet thinking of my grandmother's rape meant I could only see myself as a target. It didn't help matters that when I got on a tram and ended up chatting with a Mexican couple.

"¿Sola?" the wife repeated after I explained that, no, I wasn't on holiday with my parents or boyfriend.

"Sí," I said shyly, realizing what little confidence I now had in my original decision to come to San Juan by myself.

When I got off at my stop, the couple warned me once more to be careful.

I walked through the Castillo San Felipe del Morro completely preoccupied. I had taken most every precaution: dressing plainly, speaking Spanish, even avoiding alcohol altogether. Sure, I'd taken a risk by making that late-night Burger King run and maybe I shouldn't have told that couple that I was alone, but how safe could I be? No matter what I did, just by virtue of being a woman, I was an easy mark. Hour by hour, I became paralyzed with fear.

By the end of my first day in Puerto Rico, I almost couldn't think. I forgot that the sun set earlier there than it did back home, so I found myself stranded after dark. I had walked the two miles from my hotel to Old San Juan in the light of day with no problem. But at night, that walk was quite a different experience. There wasn't a bus that went between my hotel and Old San Juan, so I could either walk back or take a cab. I chose to walk.

The walk to the hotel was one of the most terrifying of my life, partially because it wasn't fully lit, but mainly because I had worked myself up into such a frenzy. Every man I passed was a potential predator. I entertained every sordid possibility until I just couldn't take it anymore. I ended up shitting myself—literally. Humiliated, I tried my best to control my movements so my shit wouldn't spread any more than absolutely necessary during the last leg of my journey.

Too embarrassed to take the elevator, I took the stairs to my room. I immediately threw myself into the bathroom. I peeled off my underwear, plopped the shit in the toilet, flushed it, and buried my underwear in the garbage can. I topped it off with a plush layer of toilet paper. Then I took a long, hot shower.

As I scrubbed myself clean, I thought about how this was what it meant to be a woman in an unjust world. We must fear for our lives, yet we can't let that fear consume us as it consumed me that night. We must learn to tame that fear and fight for a culture that doesn't make fear a given part of womanhood.

NICOLE
MCCARTHY

Thursday afternoon. 4pm.

The farmhouse is quiet. She beat him home from work.

she could run this time—
Her pulse palpitates as she thinks about how quickly she could
pack up what's hers.

The bathroom would be easy— grab the load of laundry from
the night before. Her mom could give her another toothbrush.
She can leave the Ross variety kitchenware, dirty in the sink.

The bedroom— they shared a twin and didn't sleep on sheets.

She could snatch her clothes by the hangers—sweaters, bras,
dresses uprooted, fainting in her arms

She'd crawl on worn knees to clear out the attic—

pupils dilated, humming in her ears, high on the thought of
leaving.

She would need a whole day. She could take tomorrow off, or
next Friday.

She thinks about striping the framed pictures from the shelves
but rocks kick up the driveway
followed by the roar of an offroad muffler.

*

Thursday afternoon. 4pm.

The farmhouse is quiet. She beat him home from work.

Her pulse palpitates as she thinks about how quickly she could
pack up what's hers.

The bathroom would be easy— grab the load of laundry from
the night before. Discard his hickorys and long johns on dirty
tiles. Her mom could give her another toothbrush.
She can leave the Ross variety kitchenware, dirty in the sink.
[but maybe she should wash them first?]

The bedroom— they shared a twin and didn't sleep on sheets.
They never had sheets.
 At night they could hear farm mice racing back & forth

She could snatch her clothes by the hangers—sweaters, bras,
dresses uprooted, fainting in her arms
A trail of socks to the car

She'd crawl on worn knees to clear out the attic—her asylum of
200 square feet

pupils dilated, humming in her ears, high on the thought of
leaving.

she would need a whole day. She could take tomorrow off, or next Friday. That's what she'll do. She'll take next Friday off.

She thinks about striping the framed pictures from the shelves
Cutting his body out—
but rocks kick up the driveway
followed by the roar of an offroad muffler.

*

Thursday afternoon. 4pm.

The farmhouse is quiet. She beat him home from work.

Her pulse palpitates as she thinks about how quickly she could pack up what's hers.

The bathroom would be easy— grab the load of laundry from the night before. Discard his hickorys and long johns on dirty tiles. Her mom could give her another toothbrush.
She can leave the Ross variety kitchenware, dirty in the sink.
An army of beer cans crowd the stove, drained & defeated.

Mental notes she collected tells her what movies are his & what are hers; what furniture is his & what is hers; what memories are his & what are hers.

The bedroom— they shared a twin and didn't sleep on sheets.
They never had sheets.
At night they could hear farm mice racing back & forth while he was inside of her

She could snatch her clothes by the hangers—sweaters, bras,

dresses uprooted, fainting in her arms
A trail of socks to the car

She'd crawl on worn knees to clear out the attic—her asylum of 200 square feet
books stacked collecting webbing and rodent droppings

pupils dilated, humming in her ears, high on the thought of leaving.

She would need a whole day. She'll take next Friday off. Would she need help? Can she ask for help?

She thinks about striping the framed pictures from the shelves
Cutting his body out—[can she ever cut his body out?]
but rocks kick up the driveway
followed by the roar of an offroad muffler.

*

Thursday afternoon. 4pm.

The farmhouse is quiet. She beat him home from work again.

Her pulse palpitates as she thinks about how quickly she could pack up what's hers.

The bathroom would be easy— grab the load of laundry from the night before. Discard his hickorys and long johns on dirty tiles. Sweep makeup and tampons and razors into safeway bags. Her mom could give her another toothbrush.
She can leave the Ross variety kitchenware, dirty in the sink.
An army of beer cans crowd the stove, drained & defeated, from last Friday. Flies circle the used tinfoil & tongs left to rot.

Steaks marinating in the fridge next to her coffee creamer are
waiting for their Friday night debut. Empty glass bottles clink a
celebration in the recycling bin.
In the living room mental notes she collected tells her what
movies are his & what are hers; what furniture is his & what is
hers; what memories are his & what are hers. The loveseat can
stay; the smell of jim beam breeds in its fibers.

The bedroom— they shared a twin and didn't sleep on sheets.
They never had sheets.
At night they could hear farm mice racing back & forth while
he was inside of her
as she watched the digital clock blink

She could snatch her clothes by the hangers—sweaters, bras,
dresses uprooted, fainting in her arms
A trail of socks to the car
[maybe she'd leave her wardrobe & start over?]

She'd crawl on bruised hands & worn knees to clear out the
attic—her asylum of 200 square feet
books stacked collecting webbing and rodent droppings

pupils dilated, humming in her ears, high on the thought of
leaving. Of finally leaving.

She would need a whole day.

but
maybe she could stay—
maybe she should stay—

She thinks about striping the framed pictures from the shelves
Cutting his body out—[can she ever cut his body out?]

but rocks kick up the driveway
followed by the roar of an offroad muffler.

*

Thursday afternoon. 4pm.

The farmhouse is quiet. She beat him home from work again.

Her pulse palpitates as she thinks about how quickly she could
pack up what's left of hers.

The bathroom would be easy— grab the load of laundry from
the night before. Discard his hickorys and long johns on dirty
tiles. Sweep makeup and tampons and razors into safeway bags.
Her mom would give her another toothbrush.

She can leave the Ross variety kitchenware, dirty in the sink,
keeping the broken mason jars company.
An army of beer cans crowd the stove, drained & defeated,
from another Friday. Flies circle the used tinfoil & tongs left to
rot. A steak marinates in the fridge next to her coffee creamer
waiting for its Friday night debut. Empty glass bottles clink a
celebration in the recycling bin.

In the living room—
the loveseat can stay; the smell of jim beam breeds in its fibers.
He'll burn the bookshelf. A sacrificial offering for his weekly
bonfire.

The bedroom— they shared a twin and didn't sleep on sheets.
They never had sheets.
At night they could hear farm mice racing back & forth while

he was inside of her
chew & liquor on his tongue
a glass of jim beam sweats on the nightstand
as she watched the digital clock blink & blink & blink
another night of using her body as a lure, trading sex for
    sobriety

She could snatch her clothes by the hangers—sweaters, bras,
dresses uprooted, fainting in her arms
A trail of socks to the car
[maybe she'd leave her wardrobe & start over?]

She'd crawl on bruised hands & worn knees to clear out the
attic—
books stacked collecting webbing and rodent droppings

pupils dilated, humming in her ears, high on the thought of
leaving. Of finally leaving.

She would need a whole day.

She thinks about striping the framed pictures from the shelves
Cutting his body out—[can she ever cut his body out? Can his
body ever not be a part of her body?]
but rocks kick up the driveway
followed by the roar of an offroad muffler.

*

Thursday afternoon. 4pm.

The farmhouse is quiet.

207

Her pulse palpitates as she quickly packs up what's hers.

The bathroom was easy— grabbed the load of laundry from
the night before. Discarded hickorys and long johns on dirty
tiles. Swept makeup and tampons and razors into safeway bags.

She left the Ross variety kitchenware, dirty in the sink.
An army of beer cans crowd the stove, drained & defeated,
from the last Friday.

In the living room—
the loveseat stayed. the couch stayed. the bookcase stayed.

The bedroom—
she snatched her clothes by the hangers—sweaters, bras, dress-
es uprooted, fainting in her arms
A trail of socks to the car
her trunk an open mouth- ready for more

She crawled on hands & knees to clear out the attic—
freed books from webbing and rodent droppings

pupils dilated, humming in her ears, high on the act of leaving.
Of finally leaving.

She needed a whole day off. She took a whole day off.

She striped the framed pictures from the shelves
cutting his body out
before rocks ever kick up the driveway.

Blueprint #3

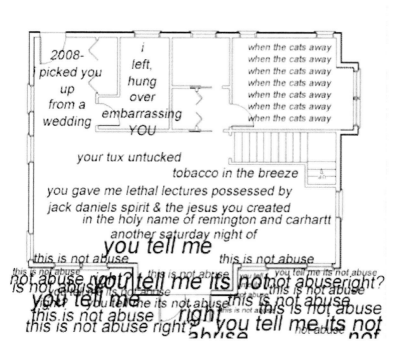

2008-
picked you
up
from a
wedding

i
left,
hung
over
embarrassing
YOU

when the cats away
when the cats away
when the cats away
when the cats away
when the cats away
when the cats away
when the cats away

your tux untucked

tobacco in the breeze

you gave me lethal lectures possessed by
jack daniels spirit & the jesus you created
in the holy name of remington and carhartt
another saturday night of
you tell me
this is not abuse   this is not abuse
this is not abuse
not abuse you tell me its notnot abuseright?
is not abuse you tell me its not abuse
you tell me its not abuse this is not abuse
this is not abuse   this is not abuse
this is not abuse right? right? you tell me its not
abuse not

ASHLEY MIRANDA

missing time

aliens come into my room and abduct me (insert childhood memory here)

aliens come into my room and stand over me (insert childhood memory here)

aliens take me and probe me (insert childhood memory here)

aliens steal my time aliens steal my mind (insert childhood memory here)

aliens keep visiting me (insert childhood memory here)

aliens keep restraining me (insert childhood memory here)

aliens steal my memory (insert childhood memory here)

aliens steal my identity (insert childhood memory here)

LEZA
CANTORAL

Toilet

You say you need to pee. I laugh and say too bad, and I keep
sitting on your lap. Your face turns to stone. You push me off
and drag me by the hair to the bathroom.
"You are going to be my toilet."
You force your cock into my mouth. Your urine sprays down
my throat. My tongue pickles in your brine. Urine fumes fill my
nostrils. One gulp is one too many.
I pull away from your cock and your grasp. I cough and cough.
I look at the toilet and I look at you. The toilet bowl looks like
one big antiseptic mouth—open just for you.
I am not white porcelain.
I am not made for you.

Zombie

The pills and the liquor don't mix.
I am tied up in your bed. This sex game has become a nightmare. I don't know what is going on. You fuck me in the ass while I babble incoherently.
I wake up the next morning like a zombie—hollowed out.
My body is not my own anymore because my body was yours last night and last night is like a videocassette that got taped over with white noises.
I've been lobotomized from my own orgasm.

DANIELLE
PERRY

A Prayer to St Dymphna

a golden charm of st dymphna
her name at the top
and at the bottom:
pray for us

--

she was just a girl
when her mother died
and her father - so lost
in his grief - decided
he would marry her instead

when she heard this was to happen
she ran, she ran, she ran
and he chased her

when he found her
he swung his sword
and took her head clean off

--

i found the charm (where?
i remember so much
but not this)
and looked up the story

i read it, and the feeling
of serendipity engulfed
my body, no longer the little girl
one that (why?) drew him

--

st dymphna, patron saint
of the mentally ill,
whose father tried to marry her,
pray for us

(Previously published on *The Fem*)

CLAUDIA CORTESE

The Red Essay

1) Setting: The barn. Sometimes, I can't remember if there were
stars, fall air clear or smoky,

                    the shape of the moon's face.

2) I read Perrault's moral to my students: *Attractive, well-bred
young ladies should never talk to strangers,*

                *for if they should, they may well provide dinner for the
wolf.*

4) Afterward, Bill died, and I was glad. Afterward, he sang Meat-
loaf to me and I held him and

                    laughed.

1.5) Other times, I can see the barn door wide open, grass below
soaked in starlight. I could have

    screamed or clawed. I dreamt saltwater
    taffy, sister's sticky kiss, how we kicked
    pigeons with our skirts over our heads.

    I worried about hurting him, that he'd feel rejected.

3) I said, *Let's go back to the house. I'm cold. Please.* Bill whispered, *It won't take long. I won't go in all the*
                    way. We negotiated. What do you name that?

6)   Angela Carter writes, *The wolf is carnivore incarnate, and he's as cunning as he is ferocious . . . If a wolf's eyes*
        reflect only moonlight, then they gleam a cold and unnatural green, a mineral, piercing color. If the benighted traveler spots those luminous, terrible sequins stitched suddenly on the black thickets, then he knows he must run.

2.5) After I read the Perrault quote, a female student says, *When a slut at a party gets drunk, it's different*
        than being attacked in a park. The class murmurs in agreement.

5)   I didn't compare myself to women choked and beaten,
        cut from the night and left to pavement.

                    To compare, one must have a basis for
comparison—
                    to know the common denominator.

7)   I bought a stack of poetry books at AWP. A wolf stalks speaker after speaker. Sometimes he
        hunts her, his spittle gleams like a knife. Other times, he awakens her animal body. They grow
        tufted and furred—they sniff and paw and wild and oh it's so
            good to be beastly be free.

8)   If we say he is evil dress him in fangs and lice tell our daughters don't stray from the path carry

    mace and listen beyond heel clicks hold your keys like a weapon don't enter the empty lot if we

tell ourselves we can keep him out by staying at the hearthside
lanterns burning like yellow eyes

in each window if we blame beer and red laughter how she
glittered his way the look that invited

him in then we can say: it *cannot* happen to me, I can't be a
victim, and I am never the wolf.

The Trauma Essay

1)   I wanted to tell you Tereus seized Philomela's tongue with pliers, she garbled a word like *father*,
        he flung the muscle to the floor, fish gasping, blood-sexed, and hid her tongueless in the fungus-dark of the forest so she'd never tell. She braided purple with red, a rug woven of what he did, which I hoped would symbolize my twining essays: I the weaver, old wife sayer—my grand mythical claim!—but when I wrote Philomela's tale I couldn't bear it I don't know how else to say this—the assault turned on me.

17) At night the corpse party
       recurred: my mother—

       dismayed by guests she didn't invite
       but too polite in that white-bread way

       to ask them to leave—
       served biscuits and milk

       for brunch, cold
       cabbage soup at lunch.

4) Why would I request you read that?

3) Type this into your computer: guardianlv.com/2014/04/ku-klux-klan-leader-busted-having-sex-
   with-black-male-prostitute

_) Small fires in the sky, not stars but scars—history's bright traces.

7) A voice can be all cuts, can piano an animal
   in the book of mouths, can be a mouth
   from which the words are written, from which
   the words are screamed.

2) *What one destroys, one eventually idealizes,*
   writes John Ebersole in a poetry review

   I read at my Macbook one morning while drinking
   fair trade coffee sweetened with Stevia.

   He means Europeans found God and Truth in the forest
   only after they'd destroyed most of it,

   and I think of Black men in America,
   how my Pan-African Studies professor in college said whites
   envied Africans—

   their beauty their bodies their perceived virility —and I
   thought
   he was crazy, now I'm not sure

   he was—

5) When whitegirl
   me bought a Eurorail pass,
   woke every three days
   to a different
   dusk—some shot
   with blood, others
   thin pinks fining
   the horizon,
   each sky felt
   like the first—

6) in fetish, my world became real.

12) The ghost at the center of each life—
    sun redglassing the ice, snows
    broken and then unbroken and then
    bootprints filling with white—

13) *All forms of mourning . . . communicate their own incompleteness.*

14) I tried to seal the holes—stopped wearing clothes with
zippers or buttons,
    chewed with my mouth shut, sipped through straws.

15) His suit jacket hung on my door, bright as a shark in black
water.

_) *unforgettable . . . because it cannot be remembered, recounted—*

16) When the sun ribbed through blinds,
        I felt stitched to my sheets. Imagine a cedar
            split to pieces, still rooted:
        tree in a jar that seals out seasons.

_) Like a patient whose illness is cured and the symptoms
      remain.

10) The story I need to tell: I went to the barn with Bill, I said no,
he said I won't stick it in all the
      way, I said okay and felt myself split, and in the every-night
      after, I lay in bed alone, said no, and he said I won't stick it in
      all the way, and I said okay, and *Now the pain is my pleasure 'cause*
      nothing could measure, sings Rihanna, and Bone says, *I couldn't*
      stop my father from beating me, but I was the one who masturbated, I
      did that, and Grey says, *There is always the woods between here and*
      the party.

18) I know the corpses,
      though I never dreamt them.
      The real dream of salt
      across windowsill, fire-
      veined door, lost girl codes—

8)   I told myself 17-year-old me burglared
      a nitrous tank from a dentist's office

      with two dudes I'd only known for a few minutes
      ballooned the night away

      because I'd been raped once
      or because my mother's economy of guilt

      her mouth all switchblades

11) *The most powerful and subtle forms of forgetting are narrative memory*
and history.

9) That's a lie: the because a coaster I dipped
    down its belly-up edge of fun

    the because like leaping to water
    body breaking in lakeskin

Girlhood

When my sister told me the man
who'd raped me killed

himself, I felt more joy
than I had ever felt before.

KELLEY
O'BRIEN

Seeing Red

Two and a half months
after the day with the van
and the torn clothes, the pain
and the man, I awake
with blood dried
on my thighs, my nightgown
stuck to me like an adhesive
that will never heal.

I can see the browned-red,
the street lamp outside my window
a spotlight on the evidence.

The blood pours down my thighs
as the tears do from my face,
leaving tiny rivulets behind me,
a trail of elapsed time.

In the bathroom, after
the waves of cramps finally
subside, I glance behind me

and I swear I see a tiny baby
lying curved in the bend of
the toilet.

(Previously published in *Psychic Meatloaf*)

Mother Wondering If Her Daughters are Growing Up Too Soon

We were young and we wondered
if it was wrong to dance *en pointe*
on the thighs of our father's mechanic.
he was thirty and his teeth were white,
cancerous and constantly in transit,
mapping our curls and our blushes
with another stressed night.
We were only children and couldn't
have appeared thoughtful in our high heels
and lipstick and mini-skirts. But our mechanic
would take our hands and he would smile
and tell us it was the theory of evolution
and at a seconds notice we would spill
silk from our balcony and stain our sheets
a brilliant shade of scarlet.

(Previously published in *Gloom Cupboard*)

JESSICA LYNN SUCHON

After Eden

Would it have mattered if I said no? No
one considers the reason for the bleeding of the daughter,

only that I bleed. I wander, bone of bone. Yes, both mortar
         & pestle. Grind finer, finer –

Who told you that you were naked?

He touched me.
I knew.

Is it true you feared making a god of me? Please,

         when I close my eyes, no whisper or tongue
flickering – blackened wick against the bow of my ear. See me

like this: sinner without sin, girl who knew
no better. More than what I am good for, than bruised
         fruit cursed to know loss & loss &

Eve Talks to Me About Loss

His rib. Always another body
inside my body. I was nothing,

then made from another, then another
made inside of me.

How could I have known
he would force his way in?

It had never happened
like that before.

I tasted war in the sweat
on his palms.

I bit his thigh
when it pinned my arm.

I cried.

It did not end.

To explain the bruises
on his leg he told
his friends I was wild.

We asked nothing & still
so much of each other, it gnawed
at us in our sleep. Yes, I confess

I saw myself in him.

I bled. He liked it.

He would smile when I panicked.

His laugh like a carving knife.

I have played the role of battered
girl before. I was comfortable with him.

When he hurt me, I hurt
him back.

I should have left, but

I stayed, learned to like it. I never
called it what it was, believed
in his goodness & my own.

maybe there is no name
for a want that resists itself.

He knew the worst parts of me & gave them
a home. I let him summon
the broken in me.

Sometimes home is fractured
bone we inherit and set.

We learn
to ignore the ache.

Of course we both became
what we promised we were
all along   *&* when it ended

I defended him & all those
secrets stretched between us
like leathered skin of a dead
thing.

It was already dead.
The thing was already dead.

Gaslight

We started fucking in places we could hide:
the winter-stomped wheat field, behind

        a stranger's barn. I saw rain
on the windshield, realized love was empty –

an eggshell, the wet rind of an orange.
I could not admit this. Did I think he enjoyed hurting

me? No
        and yes, and no.

I wanted to believe
        an answer was tangled in the blankets.

If we stripped ourselves bare
we could find it and forget our hate

for each other's bodies. There is no forgiveness.
We are still empty. He says I remember it all wrong,

but it happens again, and it happens
again he comes home drunk,

       knocks me to the ground and tells me to beg,
and we start fucking

in places we can hide: the winter-stomped wheat
field, behind a stranger's barn, he knocks me to the ground

and says I remember it all wrong.
                  He comes home drunk. There is no forgiveness.

I could not admit this. I wanted to believe.
       He comes home drunk, still empty.

Yes. I saw rain. He tells me no.
He says I remember it all wrong.

The Good Girl

On Sundays, a man carves
    roast beef at brunch and blood

    slips across the teeth
        of the carving knife. The lawns

        are always manicured
          key lime, trimmed

down to almost
    nothing. Fathers

    sleep with nannies
        and get found out.

        Summers I sleep in, wear lace
          -trimmed pajamas. Peonies

scent the air with sweet
    sickly pink and I sip

my coffee black, stare
at my shrinking hands

when I un-noose dresses
from their hangers.

A country club daughter
never wears pants to dinner.

I say my prayers. I cross my legs.
My therapist asks why

I am so sad when I have it so
good.
She wants to know why

I can't be more
like the other girls,

say please, say thank you, learn
to speak when spoken to.

The year goes on like this: my
hands
shake. I cry when I am

touched, have dreams the boy
who used to live next door takes me

for a walk. The therapist tells me
sometimes young girls,

they get their hearts broken.
I become a shadow.

Most days I open the window
  and find an unkindness

    of ravens storming the sky.
      The swans on the lake

       stretch their milky necks
        and hunch over their nests
like soldiers in a quiet
  moment of surrender.

STACI R. SCHOENFELD

Two Objects and a Girl

I.

At breakfast the girl spits out gazelle fur with every sip of tea. It clings to the walls, her saliva like glue. Gets stuck between her teeth. At night she coughs up more hair balls than the cat.

She's all instinct and scent. Smells too much of her father. He's been sniffing around. Her fur has come in and her ears grow long. She's skittish. On guard.

The girl's mother hires a dressmaker to cover her daughter's changed form, but the woman doesn't have patterns that fit the four-legged creature standing before her. She advises the mother to fashion a bed out of straw. Make the girl comfortable. *What else can you do?*

The girl knows. But her long tongue can't wrap itself around the word *flee*. The other girls call her wild and the teacher leashes her to the treadmill in gym. Over and over she runs the same course, clenches her teeth against tongue and tastes blood.

II.

One day, just like that, the girl sheds her fur. Her ears recede until they could no longer be seen, and she starts humming a lot. Her head narrows at the top and widens at the base and when struck, sounds a hollow thunk. Inside—a constant drone. She walks as though travelling through liquid gone thick and viscous.

At night, when the girl's father comes to her bed, he complains of stings.

She pedals her bike around town. Flowers bend toward her as she passes and she aches to bathe in their yellow dust. The girl is last sighted near the bus station.

The people who saw her that day swear she shimmered like a hot-road mirage. She was there and then she wasn't and the seat of her bicycle was swathed in bees.

(Previously published in *Muzzle*)

AGNES
VITTSTRAND

Excerpt from "Give them no names"
translated by Freke Räihä

I can lie so that they become truth.
I can crawl beneath reality.
I can suck dark gray turbid root slime.
The silt sludge, forced beneath the surface
after I have been forced beneath the surface.
Beneath the surface below the surface under.
New foundation persistently a new below.
The marshes tear the eyes with filth.

Daddy finds new depths in the mind.
Daddy forces someone beneath the fright.
Drown myself in the hard silt of bedrock.
I am not responsible for my thoughts.
Everything is daddy's, nothing I can grasp.
Death of memories, the blackened panic out.
These words should not be beautiful.

I can swallow the dark slime's root slime's silt.
I can lick the rim and stop being.
I can like that it is still the same.

I can rejoice at my darkness of memory.
I can rejoice at these abilities.
Beneath the surface is another surface.

JASON PHOEBE RUSCH

Manhood

Sometimes, masturbating as a teenager, I imagined male thighs (in place of my slim girlish ones), a cock (my own.) Sometimes, weeping, I imagined cutting off my clit, not to replace it, but for the comfort a lack of sensation would bring. Still I don't know what I felt, feel: my own electric strangeness or my father moving through, inside me, become me, so that the source, diffuse, cannot be pointed at, though I am its fucked locus, a whorl of trash collected ebbing in the sea. In the thrift store, I allow myself to contemplate buying a seventies-style man's button-down, then smell my father's cigarettes and return the shirt on its hanger to the rack, hands shaking. *I won't apologize for being a man*, my father said to me once, after telling me I was an attractive two-year-old, after explaining the effect of my best friend's tits on his eyeballs-

then shared a story he'd heard on NPR
about a woman taking T, how she began
to sexualize the gleaming hoods
of cars, how did he know how did he
know how did
he know
so many years
before me-

and he never did. Apologize. Apologize. That was my job. Children, like dogs, don't talk. I started talking late, little pale-haired, glazed-eyed pet, and my first word was sorry. I told myself I was telling myself a story about my story, disremembered my own bedroom into a chamber of searing light. Elided years of time into an opiate fog. My father told me a story about his boyhood, his own gerbils who he stuffed into a mason jar filled with water, flung far afield into the woods skirting the park. Woman was formed as foil for man, as jar for shame. I don't know which shame is worse: the pleasure of being an object, or the pleasure of objectifying. Cum on me, I tell men. Cum all over my tits. Fuck me breathless. I'll live vicariously through both our bodies, neither mine.

LEAH
MUELLER

Hitchhiker

Sixty-five miles from Baton Rouge
she stood on the interstate with her thumb
in the air, and a Datsun pickup truck
with Louisiana plates pulled to a stop beside her,
then stood idling on the gravel covered shoulder
of the road, while the driver motioned
for her to come inside.
She climbed into the passenger seat,
carefully, holding a duffel bag,
hastily crammed full of sundresses
and underwear, a spare pair of shoes
and seventy dollars, all the money
she owned. Her boyfriend was still asleep
in their third floor walk up apartment
in the lower Garden District, passed out on the futon
in the New Orleans heat, eighty degrees
at nine o-clock in the morning
with three quarts of beer in the refrigerator
and a note waiting for him when he awakened.
He would scream and break the furniture, perhaps
but somehow she doubted this,
he only did these things when he had an audience.

She carefully pulled her skirt over her knees
as she crouched inside the cab,
but the man noticed
and looked away, asked her name
and where she was going: She said Texas
and then a bus to Mexico,
buses were a lot cheaper down there
but until then, she had to hitchhike.
He told her it was dangerous,
and she was lucky he had picked her up
instead of some deranged nut,
and if she wrote down his address,
she could send him a postcard
to let him know she had arrived safely.
She scribbled his name and address
on a torn piece of paper from her purse,
then shoved the purse inside her duffel bag,
and zipped them both securely.
He wanted to know things:
Was she a student? Did she like music?
How long had she lived in the South?
She said hadn't been there long
and certainly didn't intend to stay much longer,
she was fleeing from her boyfriend
to see her mother, who lived the life of a boozy
American ex-patriot in San Miguel Allende
in a large house with lots of rooms
she could wander in, while she figured out
what to do next. She was twenty two
and worked at a waitress job in the Quarter,
when she failed to report for her shift
her boss would just hire someone else.
After an hour, the driver pulled over
and said he had to take a leak,

and would return shortly, and she watched
as he disappeared into a clump of bushes
a few hundred feet from the shoulder
of the road, and a lull fell over everything
except for the anonymous, metallic thumping
of car wheels as everyone headed to Baton Rouge.
Finally the man called her name
and she pushed the door of the truck
against the humid gusts of air
so she could hear him better, and he said
he had found a bird's nest with three eggs,
and she had to see it, because it was perfect.
She moved slowly forward
as he appeared from behind the bushes,
pressed the blade of a pocketknife against her throat
and pushed her to the ground,
not roughly, but firmly, as if she was a dog
and he was making her kneel to do tricks.
He told her that he wanted her,
and that she should suck him
and all of it would be over quickly.
He guided her throat to his penis
with the edge of the knife
and she placed her mouth there in a daze
then stopped, unable to continue.
"Go on" said the man, and he looked around
for a moment, but no one was watching.
The cars continued to hurtle past,
and mostly she was filled with rage
at herself, for wasting her life,
all twenty two years of it,
now she was going to bite it next to a highway
in Louisiana, and it wasn't fair.
It was completely impossible

for all of it to come to this-
so without even thinking, she bit his penis
as hard as she could, brought her teeth down
on the pulpy flesh, with all the force
of her jaw, because she had heard
that rapists kill their victims
even if they submit, perhaps more often
that way, but she wasn't completely sure
if that was true, or if she had only imagined it.
The amazing thing was, the man didn't
collapse on the ground afterward-
he gained more strength instead,
and stood above her,
he waved his knife in the air and said
"I really should kill you now"
but just as rapidly, he subsided
and stood absolutely still,
staring at his member as if it was a sick child
and he a concerned parent.
"I'm going now" he said softly,
"Stay right where you are.
Remember, I can throw knives."
He walked cautiously through the brush
to his vehicle, opened the passenger door
and hurled the woman's duffel bag
into the gravel on the side of the road-
and then, struck by a sudden recollection,
scooped it back up, slammed it into the cab
and drove away rapidly with her sundresses
and her underwear and her seventy bucks.
She waited until she was certain he was gone
and he wouldn't return, before she
finally crawled out of the bushes
and began to run,

even though she had nothing to do
except go back to the highway
and stick her thumb out again.

LAUREN
DAVIS

Camargue Horse Knows

You feed the fenced white horse
straw bits found at your feet.
So large, I protest he'll eat my hand

if I try. *Don't curl your fist*, you say.
Open palmed. I find a lengthy weed,
hold it out far as if it might catch flame.

He stomps, tosses his head, backs away.
You scared him, you tell me. *He thinks
it's a whip.* I try to coax him back, explain.

Remember when you first offered me
your long, willing body—the gift
an instinct. I shook at the threat of it.

The horse returns to you, eager
to receive from those unguarded.

MW MURPHY

I Never Tell My Mother

I never tell my mother. It was my shame to keep only me to blame. My shame, my blame till now.

Crushing heavy hands on my slender throat tightening pressing so tight no screams can escape my sixteen-year-old lips. My head thrust back under steering wheel. My long hair tangled in his thick fingers, which pull. There right in the front seat he pushes so hard against me flattening my chest so I almost can't breathe. My smallish breasts crushed by his weight. In my eyes come quick flashes scenes of my short life. The sudden sick realization that my obit will be a small bottom line on last page of newspaper. "Unknown girl's body, bruised and raped, found deep in woods."

I shake my head and try to mouth "no". I fight anew in this moment against him though he has already claimed me with his thrashing member. But as it grows flaccid and recedes I pull myself in one powerful moment free of the tyranny of his will. Grasping handle of car door, I yank it open and run. Run through the darkening woods. Damp mud soft where my bare feet almost sink into it. Leaving impressions for police to decipher sometime later. I can hear crushing of leaves behind me growing louder. Know he is following. I run. I try to run faster in the dark, just glimpsing branches enough, by filtered shadowed light of moon, to escape most. But a cluster of low hanging brambles from a tree vine scratches against my face. I want to yell out shrill in pain but, now in total self-preservation mode, stifle all sounds before they reach my throat. I can hear his heavy breathing getting closer louder. Then suddenly there is the road and lights of cars and he recedes behind bushes leaving only me.

In the hospital ER cubicle I wait, shivering under a rough cotton gown so loose I wrap its straps around me twice, and swing my skinny legs back and forth, back and forth. I can hear them laughing how "yes there are sperm on the slide, but maybe they are from my boyfriend". I feel my face growing hot because I sense they don't believe me. Somehow I was wrong and brought this all on me. Finally they give me pills to take and directions how. I mustn't have a child. I am a child. My next period bleeds clots and lasts ten days.

And again and again in the police station I am raped again emotionally. Over and over they want to hear my story. Each new officer crowding around the table and a certain red-haired one asks me for my number when the captain leaves the room to get a glass of water.

I never tell my mother. I talk to a youth counselor. The police have found him and brought him in. She wants me to bring charges. I am scared nervous. But she is insistent says this will bring me closure. I balk at the pages of forms. Finally, in a moment feeling numb, force my shaking hands to sign.

Weeks later, months really, my phone starts ringing incessantly. Unknown male voices threatening me. Taunting me they say that they know who I am. that I am a slut, a whore, I wanted it. Finally, in one very late night call, they say he is after all the Chief of Police's son. Terrified, my eyes wider then when as a child a Fourth of July firecracker exploded next to me so close I could feel its heat and smell its stench, I hang up the phone.

I do not answer when my counselor calls. I do not go to court. I never tell my mother.

I never speak of it.

KATIE
CLARK

6th sense

apparently,
      every seven years we become a new body.

i'm not sure if this is true
     but today i started counting.
        fact:
        it is hard to mourn a moment
you can't remember.
   fact:
   i lied about having seen the sixth sense until last year.

         (i looked it up on wiki-
pedia in 7th grade)
  fact:
  bruce willis was dead the whole time
   (surprise)   fact: fact:
       he didn't know   been there.
  fact:
  i was alive for thirteen hours without knowing

fact:

i fell asleep

                                                            fact:
                                                             i
woke up with you next to me
                    fact:
                    i had different clothes on   & body aches
        fact:
        & you had me walk you home
                (& got hair dye on my favorite sweater)
                                                            fact:
                                                            you
kissed me that morning
                        fact:
                        bloodspitbloodspitbloodspit
fact:
that night i was supposed to bring you a copy of national geo-
graphic fact:

                    i didn't
        fact: fact:
        i threw up & slept in my friend's bed   i think i
didn't sleep
                            fact:
                            the first thing i did was cut my
hair   fact:

        but now
every time it gets long enough
                                        to run my fingers
through
        i need it gone
fact:
you told me while drinking a cup of tea
                                        fact:
                                        my palms are
shaped like the spit
                you left on the lid/

                                        me
                                                    fact:
                                                    there are still
mornings i wake up
        and it has just happened
                                        fact:
                                        but it isn't every morning
anymore
            & somedays this feels like

                                                    healing

fact:
                                                                            it
is not over
                fact:
                everyday   i am bruce willis realizing
    fact:
    i don't get to be alive like i was alive before
                                                        all of
your hands/mouths/
            fact:
            sometimes i lie beside my partner   & feel like a
ghost
    fact
    sometimes i lie beside my partner & you are a ghost there

fact:
sometimes i lie beside my partner   & i am so there

& you aren't
                fact:
                this is happening more & more
                                                fact:
                                                it's been
seventeen years since
        bruce willis realized

                              fact:
                              he's become 2.42 bodies
since
        fact:
        it has been 9 months since i realized
                                          fact:
                                          i am
0.107 newer
              & today that is enough

CHRISTOPH
PAUL

The Boy From Military School

His smiling face haunts me. I was thirteen. He was seventeen. In military school, rank was everything—I had none and he was a sergeant.

He had bullied me but never assaulted me. He would slam me against walls and tell me how worthless, ugly, and pitiful I was. I was too small to strike back and too scared to tell on him.

A part of me began to believe him.

By my third day in military school, my sense of self was eroding. I was scared. They shaved my head and the older boys taunted me, telling me I looked like a monkey.

I didn't respond and did my best not to cry.

Willingham was always the worst one. He enjoyed tormenting anyone weaker than him. He was not popular with the kids his age. Instead, he spent his time in the middle school dorms, supposedly to make sure we acted like good cadets. While other older kids bullied and threated for money or to display their rank, Willingham harmed us because it amused him. I remember those eyes; how angry they always looked, how happiness only appeared in them when he asserted himself over a young cadet.

I am no longer religious but I can remember praying to God to keep me safe. To please not let Willingham or anyone bigger and stronger harm me. There were many sleepless nights were I didn't hear God, but I remembered and replayed the threats of what Willingham wanted to do to me.

But I learned to sleep. My teenage body adapted to dangerous terrain like my ancestors did when hunted by predators. If you angered the wrong person, you could be woken up with socks filled with bars soap or worse.

I tried my best to be invisible, but it only made me more noticeable to Willingham.

One night while I was sleeping, Willingham shoved a broom up my rectum. I opened my eyes in pain. His awful smile and laugh still give me chills when I recall them. If I had tried to defend myself he would have just beaten me with the broomstick. He did what he did because he could. I wish I could say I got justice even in the smallest sense of the word, but I did not. There was nothing I could do. My best option to not get assaulted again was to keep it to myself.

I stayed silent for a long time, long after I left military school.

Inner screams of shame and anger only became louder. I'd drink more, I'd try different drugs—some prescribed, some I'd pick up, always looking for ways to distract myself from what happened. Even when making friends with other men, I jump back if one touches me or if I see their hands coming toward me below the waist.

What happened changed me forever. A part of me died that night. Being in therapy doesn't take the pain go away but it does help me face each day. I've been on and off of depression medication since military school.

Every day is a challenge.

Every day I make the choice to trust the people I love and to live my life.

LORA
NOUK

Trust Complex

She's 12 loosing membrane
w 18 y old boy w long eyelashes who can't be stopped mostly
unnamed & never about u
no memory only memoir "snowpussy"
mother at mental house's father's transgressions I can't want my
own
Dad's Worst Rape fuck a naturalized pet
unruled never looked back yes, SCUM = run
two shadows occur too close on the street NYPD keeps your
underwear but how long? thought the unreal mad and frozen in
blue shoes the pleasure of the hex
less/more blood She got a man She got love

ALEXIS
SMITHERS

In Defense of Helga G. Patacki

In her defense, your honor,
when someone grows up abused--
that is to say
defining lovable
as everything they are not--
you're gonna do some off the wall shit.

In her defense, your honor,
she's just a child.
which doesn't excuse the behavior but does
require us to examine it.

In her defense, your honor
she did try to get some of it out
in poems
and shrines
and collecting ever kindness
he ever gave her.
She did try.

In her defense, your honor,
she does have heart.
so much that
her knees are sticky
from the flood it creates.
And one day
she could figure out that
her feeling
is not ten sizes too big
for her too small chest.
She could figure out that
the world was just too weak
to hold her ache.

In her defense, your honor
when you like-like someone and
that is the only good in your life
you will hold onto that like-like
until you can make it love
until you can make sure it will not run away.

In her defense, your honor
she did not know that holding that long
turned to squeezing so quick.
She did not know that caring like that
would make it stop breathing.

In her defense, your honor
the prosecution is correct.
The name-calling and shoving
and spitballs and threats from
ol' betsy and the five avengers
are wrong, yes,

but, your honor, what in her life has forced her
to believe the only way to speak true
is through violence?

In her defense, your honor
if you take a look at her home life,
we all know
her family was not going to teach her
the right
way to do this.
and you can't punish her for wanting.
For longing for
the good beating
shining in the injured's chest
after years of sculpting
hearts from shit.

In her defense, your honor
no one got hurt
--permanently--,
aside from the defendant
and in her case, she won't even
realize that until years later.

In my defense, your honor
life during trauma demands language
no one wants to learn to speak.

In our defense, your honor,
you cannot blame only us for the blood
when no one answered our screaming.

HANNAH
KUCHARZAK

Anxious Diva

Today I collect a census to see who knows if I'm the man, the victim, or if I've become a human torso filled with plastic bags. The gentleman on my left says he needs more information. He asks what color my nipples are. I ask him if he, too, would like to meet my blood. He hands me his card.

My police reports are written on small, pink slips. My police reports explicitly state FOLKS WON'T LIKE TO HEAR ABOUT THIS so I talk instead about my nipples, which everyone has questions about.

My police reports have the weighty feel of fresh money from the bank. They stick together and I panic, but no, I thumb the corners and shuffle them, one two three.

Every night before bed I read my police reports. Sometimes I recreate the interrogation. Sometimes I get drunk and wonder at what point I am too drunk to be listened to. I get drunk and shout out my window. I ask the neighborhood if they can hear me say no or if that is too quiet. I yell at the neighborhood to get off of me, to stop sweating onto my skin. I wake up in the middle of the night with my police reports under my pillow. Anxious Diva, slinking wolf, please file these away, please don't tell me where they are. I want to happen upon them once when I'm not thinking, like during dinner, an applause, or my honeymoon.

(Previously published in *TYPO*)

Anxious Diva

Anxious Diva puts me up for ransom.
I ask her why I can't feel my body.
She just wanted to smell the cake up close.

Who can blame her? Herself orbitless,
disappeared? Dress sagging below the knees.
Miss Charity wearing a ski mask, no panties.

I can't touch my own body and its tremors.
If Diva wanted to give us the big kiss
we could have said goodbye. Pale bitch lips,

ghosted. Diva ties me up and swipes paint
onto my mouth, one that can neither kiss
nor confess. I will not scream. I've been here before.

I'm not sure who will pay my ransom.
I ask her what a "deadline" means.
She licks a dollar bill and presses it

to the back of my neck, to keep me from fainting.

Anxious Diva, men like me because I'm slick
commodity. Men like low risk high reward.
 They see my black lace and sigh relief. Big coins
glimmering deep in Diva's bustier. *It's okay. I still trust you.*
A painless version of myself feels ingenuous.

(Previously published in *Vagabond City*)

Anxious Diva

Ravenous and exhausted, how do I
make sex work for me? How can I coax

my own appetite in the pale blue neon
of the super-buffet advertisement?

Anxious Diva, I can get through it this time.
Enduring pleasure, they say, my, what an impossible
task that must be! I unroll my stockings—

they lie on the carpet like snake skins,
knowing what comes next. As a daughter,

I was never told my body had a history.
I can lie, as I have done, but body remembers.

I was never taught to question my duty,
never shown the manual, never told the fight
was an option, but the famished

can only fight using forks.
If my sisters weren't mute they could tell me

STOP DREAMING / THE MAN WHO LOVES YOU
IS STILL AN ANIMAL. My mute sister,
come touch me where it hurts, my

trigger buttons. Come open your blouse

and show me the bruises, you hysterical thing.
There there, it's only a nightmare, it's only a dream.

Anxious Diva, I'm dying. I'm so tired. I'm reduced
to guttural cries, to hellion screams. To being locked

in the basement, the attic, the bedroom. When I met you,

Anxious Diva, I didn't have to guess at where you'd been.
All terror-filled poise and black marble, the goddess

who gave me life. Who told me to walk to the edge
and then grabbed me by the collar. She held my earlobe
and whispered my salvation:

ONE IN FIVE WOMEN BECOME A RED ARTIFACT.
ONE IN FIVE WOMEN ARE LOUD ENOUGH
FOR THEIR STATISTIC TO BE HEARD.

Diva laughed as she rubbed my back through the dry-heaves.
She laughed when I told her my pain is a sunless shadow.
She laughed and she told me welcome home.

ANNIE
VIRGINIA

The Mother

When the DA tells me my rapist did nothing
morally wrong
under the law,
then asks my silence what I want to say,
I want to ask her how her babies are.
I want to know how she can bring children into this world
where she must read the script to someone else's
that the man who raped her did alright. He'll never sleep
one night fearful. I wonder if when she goes home at night
she can feel anger in the bones of her past lives
and this is how she keeps going.

This is a woman who never wins.
She has promised her soul to a document
written in the spit of men. Cum and coffee.
She knows the details of what he did to me.
I wonder if she'll dream about it, or if she's had to
stop dreaming. Maybe she watches her every move
to make sure she's not in danger. I didn't do that part right.
My fault. I hope when her husband touches her,
she knows his hands so well that they never morph
into the sweat-smell fists she meets in stories.

I hope her daughter does not grow up too hard
to grow into anger so it fits her. It is best she doesn't
dreamcatch for her mother. I worry about her son,
who might tiptoe around in his body bigger than he wants it,
may never know his fingers can be so soft he can hold
a heart without collapsing it. But when I told her
I hate men, she asked why. Maybe she is missing something.
I hope she is missing something.
Maybe she has always had her entire body to herself.

It Would Not Have Happened

If I had been wearing shoes that didn't slip off.
If I had not changed from my dress of the morning.
But that's not what they say.
If I had sat on my chair and not my bed.
If I'd lost my keys.
If I'd found my keys, used my pocketknife.
If I'd had one fewer glasses of wine or one more shot of
    tequila.
If less people had told me to be nice to men.
If men had been nicer.
Always and on and back.
If they had played a song worth dancing to.
If Alanna had loved me, too, all these years.
If Southern hospitality weren't stuck in my gentleman words.
If my hair were short.
If we hadn't taken the time to clean up the deck of cards.
If I'd been more tired. If I'd been more awake.
If my body weren't made of what the earth doesn't tell anyone.
If Tati had never left. If Celeste had never left.
If I'd fallen down like I did in every city in Italy.
I am grateful for every scar of prevention.

How much smaller they are.
If I'd shattered the wine glass.
If the weather weren't so nice.
If my voice hadn't stuck in my chest like a scrap of hot metal.
If I had had plans Saturday morning.
If someone had been in the hallway.
If I had loved Allison more than myself.
If boxers turned off the predator in him.
Look, this is my boy armor, it has always been.
You don't want me.
If I'd chosen a different house.
If I were sicker, if it showed.
Maybe that's just it.
If I used more wanting words when I have cursed God.
If I had ever hit anyone.
If I put my money where my mouth is.
If I'd listened when New York told me to leave.
If I had told him he was not welcome.
Kindness and manners and nonchalant.
If I had fought back.
Tall and heavy and inside and unknown.
If I said no faster.
If I had not done it wrong.
If I had done it right.

When My Girlfriend and I Swapped Rape Stories

she avoided the word altogether, still unsure
of whether she could throw him under the bus like that.
I garbled the details by using it, its blunt force.
I don't mention blood or the truest nightmare
of the hospital dirt; maybe the word comes ribbed
with all that meaning, anyway. We nurse between us
a feeling of sorry, sorry older
than our greatest grandmothers' fears, and specific
to women who love women
who have been split open.

I treat my trauma like a person
she'll never need to meet, certainly no one
who will dance between us
so we can't see how joyful the other's face is
swimming in music. I don't show her the face
that turned my breathing into a collapsing
universe. I have begged her
and my other lovers
not to show me the faces of the men

who raped them. But they always do.
My lovers won't believe
that I couldn't not kill these men.
I don't understand their need
for me to see.

My girlfriend wants children,
but I want to protect our daughter instead.
I want to protect ourselves, aged
40 and waiting for our baby to come home
without swelling. I can curl in at every siren,
but I can't watch her do the same.
Maybe she would never worry
like I do, like there are channels of underground
history dark in the marrow. But I am already old
with how I've worried and grieved. The heart
chugs itself out trying to shelter the women
in the night. Especially from a distance,
the tissue cannot stretch across the doors
to bar the entrance where men will come,
so it wraps around and round itself.

Like spun cotton candy, it sticks to

our lovers' mouths and fingers, but only
it won't let go. The fear and the men,
they won't let go.

SARAH
MADGES

PTSD President

The words unhooked the stitches in my skin, opened an old wound that gleamed bright and wet like the meat of a ruby red grapefruit. The banner on the TV read: "Trump Elected 45th President of the United States."

A shudder of recognition ran through me as I watched an echo of my assailant smile and accept the most powerful position in this country.

Exactly one month earlier, I celebrated my five-year "trauma anniversary," knocking almost-memories loose with a few too many drinks. Because I had dissociated during the rape itself, I'd never processed what happened, never filed it as a memory; it roiled just below the scrim of consciousness, ready to intrude on reality.

That night had begun on a Saturday and ended 6am Sunday, when he finally left the Berlin flat I'd been calling home for the past month. Skin tight, sore, smelling like some man and his brand of cigarettes, I took steam locomotive puffs of breath into a grocery bag, hawking clear liquid, trying so badly to puke.

We are raised to anticipate it. The "Don't Go Into the Woods" type fairytales told to us as children, allegorical lessons for girls to accept their responsibility in going out and getting themselves raped. The repetition of the crime in headlines almost routinizes it, makes it seem awful but inevitable: boys will be boys will rape girls unless the girls do something about it.

What could I have done? I said no, but not enough? I said no, but it didn't seem like I really meant it? No, one more time with feeling?

*

I left my body and didn't come back for two years. Everything not quite real, the way you float on the third glass of wine. I felt immune to pain, suffering, even death. The worst had already happened, and so I was free in a Camus kind of way, earning an absurd indifference to my life.

I approached Getting Over It methodically, Googling cycles of grief and articles about recovery and the aftershock of trauma, searching for some definitive text: What to Expect When You're Expecting to Develop PTSD. Copy & pasting sections from articles about "being a survivor" and reclaiming your body in word documents, I underlined scores of metaphors for dissociation with a sense of déjà vu drifting over me as I heard my thoughts repeated to me in someone else's voice.

How necessary they felt. The kind of thing writers share on social media with only the word "this" offered as caption.

I read that when people don't work through trauma, their body idles at a heightened state. I learned about "counterphobia," the idea of moving toward something triggering instead of away from it in order to prove to yourself you're okay.

On my own, I learned that trauma means not knowing what will set you off, but knowing that something will. It's inexplicably flinching, heart galloping in your chest, when a man gets too close to you on the subway, or brushes up against you at a concert, or looks at you from across the bar for too long. It's drinking to black-out as a way to collapse time, to live through something without the burden of its memory. It's training your body to accept a purple, thumb-shaped piece of silicone, like a thumbs up on trying to overcome PTSD! you

insert up your asshole after a day of butt plug-browsing at Babeland because you refuse to let this thing that happened to you years ago continue to limit your behavior, to get cagey about naked bodies and what they sometimes do together.

*

It's a peculiar thing, surviving sexual assault, because it's not just a personal issue: it's a crime. The legal seeps in, and the vocabulary doesn't suffice. You're tasked with quantifying an unquantifiable pain. It's like you've been robbed of the alphabet and then commanded to spell a word without any help from its letters.

And that's just when you testify. Ultimately, a stranger is responsible for defining the terms of your violation, the punishment that fits the crime. Unlike with other felonies, the victim of rape often comes under more scrutiny than the alleged perpetrator. She is asked what she was wearing, if she'd been drinking, if she's sexually active, and is she sure she wants to press charges?

The justice system submits her to another trauma, a flaying-open, re- victimization.

I never filed a report. I didn't feel empowered to seek legal recourse when the first "authority" (read: adult at the study abroad office) I consulted said "it happens all the time," and shrugged as though unimpressed. I needed to "learn not to be so nice," she said.

He tossed me around like a ragdoll, penetrating me vaginally, then anally when I rolled onto my stomach to try and block access, but even on my fifth reading of the FBI's definition, I deliberated whether mine "counted"—had I been sufficiently raped?

Besides, I didn't want to have to see him again or endure his legal team spinning the truth into a sticky web of loopholes designed to entrap and discredit me. I didn't want to square

up against all the blank faces squinting at another Girl Who Cried Rape, a drama queen willing to ruin a poor guy's life over one night of regrettable sex.

People wonder why no more than 20 percent of rapes are reported to the police—why don't the One in Four who survive come forward?—and I find myself C+Ving poignant phrases from thinkpieces in Facebook posts again.

In her essay "When Your Abuser is Elected President," published on November 9, 2016, Jody Allard summarizes the country in which she awoke that morning as one that "chose the side of the abuser in one resounding vote." She wrote: "A man who helps himself to women's bodies will lead our nation, and teach our sons what it means to be a man."

"This," I write. How do we deal with *this*.

CACONRAD

For My Boyfriend Earth
Who Was Raped And Murdered

your rapists were the last
to taste you in this world
their breath and
terror
down your
neck keeps
me up at
night but
which
page of the bible says
to burn the faggot after
you force him to give
you your pleasure
each time I drink water dropped from clouds
water they burned out of your body I cup my
hands to catch you
in the revenge dream I behead one of them
spell your name on my face with his blood
the other is begging as I choke him
his neck as soft as your neck

I pull him off his
knees check for
tattoos
is it
him is
it you
I miss
you I
love you

HILLARY LEFTWICH

The Last Night You Tried to Have Fun
(Sung to "Girls Just Want to Have Fun")

I come home in the morning light. Head stuffed with fuzz and questions, tailbone bruised from striking cold tile. You're not thinking about washing away forensic evidence when you start the shower, the water slapping your face. The feel of his dried sperm on your stomach, between your breasts, makes you gag. It's all you can do to not scrape your own skin off.

The phone rings in the middle of the night. It vibrates on your bed-side table, skittering off the edge and cracking on the floor. The brochure the victim's assault worker gave you says it's normal to feel paranoid after a sexual assault. It's normal to not feel normal. You don't feel anything as you stare outside your bedroom window. Your body is tattooed with bruises and it screams when you move. You are waiting for him. He will pound on your door and ask you if you went to the cops. He will want to silence you.

That's all they really want. Some fun. You left the bar with him. Walked to his apartment where a party was going on. In his bedroom it was dark and warm. Drumbeats and laughter from the party in his living room leaked through the closed door like muffled heartbeats. He grabbed your arms with both hands. His breath was a swarm of hornets in your face. He is catching you because you are falling. The room smeared with black. The red plastic cup with the remainder of the beer he poured for you dropped from your hands. You descended to the floor like an anchor.

Oh mother dear we're not the fortunate ones. The detective tells you about cross-examination, about being put on display while you testify on the stand. How the defense attorneys will tell the story of your guilt. For what you were wearing that night. For drinking two shots of whiskey and a beer. For meeting a guy at a bar and going home with him. You are every girl-in-a-bar joke. He tries to prepare you for the second assault. (How strong are you?)

Some boys take a beautiful girl. There is smooth tile underneath your bare ass. You open your eyes to a toilet hanging over your head, your panties shoved down to your ankles like pink shackles and your bra pulled up under your chin. Two guys from the party stand over you as they hold their cell phones in front of them, the light from the flashes on their phones blinding you. The guy you left the bar with--the guy who told you about how music saved his life and offered your son drum lessons--shoves himself inside of you over and over. He grabs your (nice tits) and smiles at his friend's phones. Paparazzi. High fives a hand. Asks you (why are you so dry?) Laughter crackles like a bonfire.

Girls, girls just wanna have fun. He is all suit and tie, staring at you as the defense attorney points in your general direction. Like it doesn't even matter where you are. He is smiling, laughing softly in response to his attorney's questions. His brown hair is combed and not a mess like you remember. He has dimples. You can see why you left the bar with him. He tells the courtroom you were both having fun. He looks at the jury and tells them it was consensual.

That you never said *NO*.

That you never said *STOP*.

That's all they really want. You can't explain how you couldn't talk. How everything was heavy, underwater. How you tried to scream but your voice was jammed in your throat. How you were awake, florescent lights, then black. Awake. Florescent. Black. How you tried pushing him off of you but your hands wouldn't lift. (She was drunk, so I let her crash at my place.) Several men and women on the jury nod their heads as they survey you, their stares scaling the length of your body. You tug down your knee-high skirt, finger the buttons on your blouse.

I want to be the one to walk in the sun. You walk out of the court-house at the same time as him, separated only by your attorneys. It is late morning and you hear him say, *there is still time to catch brunch.* You watch as he gets in the back seat of a waiting Town Car along with his parents. His father claps him on the back and his mother fixes her lipstick with her pinky finger, squinting at her reflection inside a tiny green compact. You stare just long enough to see him remove his red tie and toss it on the seat next to him like a bloodied rag. You wonder where he's going, what he will be in ten years. If his dimples will fade. You wonder what you will be. You think about going home, shutting the door, closing the blinds, and washing the feeling of guilt off of you all over again.

Oh, girls.

MILA
JARONIEC

What I Felt After Getting Raped, Redux

Both of the times I was raped, I walked away feeling lucky. Lucky for holding onto my body, lucky for making it out alive. I was making compromises with the universe. *I was raped, but not murdered.* That's good. *I could've gotten HIV, but I didn't.* That's good. I've written about this before, but back then my mind was different.

"The first thing I thought of was this bear attack video we watched in middle school, what you should do when you're about to be eaten. It was a dumb impulse but it was all I had to work with so I slowed my breathing and played dead. Curiously, it worked. He got up to use the bathroom and I stumbled out into the morning light to hail a cab, dizzy and half-clothed, trying to explain where I lived in my awful Chinese. Later, slumped in the back of the cab in my dirty t-shirt watching the tangerine rose of the sunrise spread over the city, I felt so fragile and so lucky."

This was the second time. I was 22 and teaching English in China. I had gone to the bar to meet a friend at 10 p.m. and woke up at 5:30 a.m., in a part of the city I'd never seen.

"And furious. What had given this asshole the right to touch me? To drug me and *then* touch me? It seemed like the most insulting thing, that he didn't even try. Didn't ask me, didn't even force me, just put something in my cocktail like NBD. Obviously rape isn't a sex thing, it's a power thing, but still. He had to knock me out to make it easier, like having to tranquilize a tiger before reaching out to pet it. Like he knew my body wasn't an object he should be touching but reached for it anyway."

I was trying to make sense of the rape.

"And I was exhausted, more tired than I'd ever been. Sapped of energy, spread thin like translucent wax paper. Tired like I'd never smile again, like I'd never be able to move again, just crumpled there, pasted limply to the sticky backseat. Tired and sick, dry heaving with a blinding headache, a metallic tightness in my chest and stomach, an insistent squeeze compressing my temples and my heart."

I was trying to make sense of myself.

"And incredibly annoyed. Annoyed that my top priority upon returning home was now to get tested. Annoyed that I had been clean and now there was a chance I wasn't because this guy decided to stick his penis where it didn't belong, that I had to repeatedly recount what happened to nurses with clipboards, that I had to drop a bunch of money I didn't have on finding out whether he had given me something else besides humiliation. Terrified that the HIV test might come back positive. Thanks, guy. Thanks a lot."

And I was still trying to be funny.

And use literature as medicine.

"Back at my apartment, I pulled my hair back in the mirror and examined my reflection. *I am still myself.* It was a line I pulled from *Suicide Blonde* because I didn't have the words."
And manage my expectations.

"I knew exactly what was going to happen next, and I was ready for it. *What were you wearing? How much did you have to drink?* All the inevitable questions of rape culture, the things we ask the victims because our first instinct is to examine their actions instead of the rapists'. We want to make sure she wasn't 'asking for it' before we give her our empathy. *How short was* her *skirt? Were* her *tits hanging out? What gave* him *the right?* I'll give you one guess as to which statement doesn't belong."

Make myself feel okay in the world again.

"And even though I wanted to not exist, collapse into the floor and decay, I knew I had to be strong because no one was going to be strong for me. I wasn't about to get on Skype and broadcast what happened, open up the wound and rehash the details. I knew what my parents would say, what the police would say. There wasn't anything to do except sit there and breathe, sit there and pump blood through my body, cradle every limb and feel thankful for the fact that some part of me, at least, was not damaged, the rest would heal itself."

Steel up and shut down.

"After all, what could anyone say? At best, *I'm here for you*, at worst, *I told you so*. The words would pass through but they wouldn't resonate. No one who hasn't been there can understand the horrible nothingness of it, the extent to which there's nothing to do besides just live through it because you don't have a choice, reduce it to its bare bones and digest it like everything else. Chew it and wash it down like every other thing that happens because going to pieces over it won't make it clearer, won't make it easier, won't make it anything."

There's nothing to do, the survivor who wrote this concluded.

No.

I wouldn't write it this way now.

No more quiet self-preservation. No more swallowing the reality. No more social silence. No more looking the other way. No more internalized blame. No more *this is what it's like for women*. No more I wasn't that drunk. No more *does that really count as rape?* No more thinkpieces. No more essays. No more rationalizing. No. No more.

The survivor writing this is a fighter too.

No more apologizing for having a human body. No more acceptance of rape as an existential hazard. No more feeling grateful for the minimal amount of abuse. No more "understanding" the other side. No more throwing the hands up. No more normalization of rape culture. No more *this is the way things are*. No more dissociation. No more distance.

No more discussion.

Action.

Now.

PRERNA
BAKSHI

Coming Out

12 years old.

Come here, he said. Look what I've got for you, he said. I wanted it to be a surprise, he said. I've been planning to show you for days, he said. I've made sure it pops out as soon as you unwrap it, he said. I bet you'll open your mouth as soon as you see it, he said. You might scream, he said. You might cry, he said. You might say I shouldn't have, he said. But I know you wanted it, he said. So don't be shy, he said. Come here, he said. Come and lie down with me, he said. It's under these sheets, he said. Get your head under there, he said. Start looking, he said. Don't come out until you find it, he said.

I hadn't come out
until now.

(First appeared in Sick Lit Magazine, US)

CORINNE
MANNING

Primary Sources

"Susan! Look at Susan!!"

"What's wrong?"

"You're –*Gasp*- Fading Away!"

"Oh, No!! No!!"

"Somehow the cosmic rays have altered your atomic structure… making you grow invisible!"

"How… how long will it last?"

"There's no way of knowing!!"

"Wha—what if she never gets visible again??"

"Look! I see her."

"I'm myself again! It happened so suddenly…all by itself!"

Fantastic Four Issue #1

Dissociation is a super power marked by an exceptional gift of grace and control: to exit a situation and to still be physically present; to seem present to those around you and on top of you, but to not actually be *there*. To be able to observe with a cool distance—the physical attack is not you, in fact you may be able watch it, slow and distort time; remember only what seems useful to remember. You may leave all together. You may commune with the gods. And when it's practiced correctly, the proprietor of the skill doesn't need to even initialize it. It moves like a response, a highly tuned reflex. The situation might be the cause, but disassociation is the solution. With what is lost comes something gained.

It was the blizzard of '96. It was 3 am.

Say that you're on your way to pick him up, my mom said.

Pat, my father said, *tell him I'm going to pick him up*. I didn't recognize then that he was talking to my brother's roommate. Pat, at that moment, could have been anyone. My dad turned and looked at my mom. *He says he doesn't want me to, says he's fine.* My dad has a very clear, open face that never gives away what he's actually feeling. He keeps the same expression on his face most of the time whether he's angry or sad. His eyes were pink then and his jaw bone pulsed under the skin of his cheek. He is a master of control and caution. On the morning my brother was jumped he could get by with grinding his teeth.

In a case study with a Mexican nun named Celeste, Rebecca Lester, an anthropologist, learned the following:

Celeste turned to me and said, 'Rebe, do you ever feel like you're not where you are?'

I asked her what she meant. 'I mean, do you ever kind of go away from yourself?

[...] She then went on to describe experiences she had been having for over a year where she felt as if she were leaving her body, 'as if time and space were broken' and she 'went off somewhere else': *It's like all of a sudden it gets difficult to hear what's going on around me, kind of like when you're under water, and I know I'm about to have one of these experiences…It's so peaceful. It's really beautiful. Lots of times I don't want to come back.*[i]

At some point all humans long for at least one of these abilities: to transform, to flee, and to alter. Most of the time these qualities seem completely unobtainable, the stuff of superpowers. A superpower can be any ability that is somehow above and beyond normal human ability. Celeste survived two attempted rapes, both when she was a young child. When Celeste would dissociate she felt certain she was communing with God. Comic Theorist Bradford W. Wright notes that the main draw to superheroes is the hope that a life altering ability lies within the every day American.[ii] We feel rage against injustice, and we want to believe that we'll act when offered the chance, that we will use whatever skills we have to do what the hero should do. We might not even know what this skill is but we want to believe it's waiting in us—waiting in everyone, waiting for the trigger.

"*Well Maybe they're right. Maybe I am a monster!*" The Thing

My brother is a large guy but his face has gnome-like features. It was early morning when he walked through the door with my father. There was a bandage on the back of his head. He looked at me and my mother and seemed annoyed. When my mom explained to me that he had been jumped, beaten and robbed she speculated on why he was the one. What was it about him? My brother wasn't out yet. He looked at us as if he knew this was what our conversation had been about.

My mom got up and hugged him but he didn't hug back. She started to pull at the bandage on his head and he shoved her away.

He shouted: told her to leave it alone.

I'm your mother!

My brother stiffened and looked off into the room while my mom pulled back the bandage. I moved around the side of the room to see it. I didn't need to move as quietly as I did, my brother wasn't really there. The gash stretched across the back of his head, was bloody, swollen. I could see the staples squeezing the flesh together. I didn't mean to say it, but it came out too quickly. Are you okay? My brother didn't look at anyone. He laughed.

This is how I remember my brother telling me the story of that night:

> *All the public transportation was shut down, and it was a full moon, and not so cold out. It was 1 or 2 am, but I've done that walk before at that time. It was so beautiful out, the snow was so high on either side of me and the moon was just glowing down. That's where I screwed up. I relaxed. I heard some voices, and then I heard swishy pants running behind me. I didn't turn around in time. (The sudden switch to present tense.) That's when they started hitting me with the pipes. There are two of them. They just keep hitting me and you can look at them and realize they are probably 13. I'm down on the ground, curled up. They don't know what they are doing. I manage to get my hand in my pocket and pull out my wallet and then I say 'Okay, you've made your point. Take my wallet now.' Then they ran away, like, skipping away and they shouted, we did it, we did it! I was probably their first one. I was totally wet and at first I thought it was from the snow, or from sweat but it was my blood. (It had soaked through two sweaters and three t shirts.) I walked home and I was counting the steps. Just trying to get home. I couldn't stop thinking about how they had my address. That they were going to burn down my house.*

We sat for a while after that, watching TV.

It's like, I don't even care about that. The thing that drives me crazy is how everyone keeps asking me if I'm okay. What am I supposed to say to them?

You don't say anything to anyone. You don't even need to tell them about it. No one needs to know, it won't serve them. Every superpower has its downside. In the case of dissociation, the panic that should come in the moment, waits, comes other times, comes when it's not necessary—can take over even if you're not threatened. So just be still. You will feel something, sometimes, but often you won't be able to tell what happened and what didn't. What happened and in what order.

My brother was home for two weeks. On one of the last days I walked by the bathroom. My brother was looking at himself in the mirror and told me to join him.

I stood next to him and faced the mirror. In the reflection I couldn't tell if we looked alike. I made my face calm to look like his. We both stood there, looking like our father.

He told me that I had to learn how to look and walk. He pushed his dark eyebrows closer to his eyes and his cheeks rose in response. He managed to spread his eyelids open wide. He clenched his jaw. I laughed. He released the face.

Do it. So I did. He is nine years older and back then I still followed his direction.

He told me to make it angrier, to look like someone's just messed with me and I killed them, like I might kill the next person who bumped into me. We laughed at my face. *This is what you have to do. Then people will look at you and think, Oh boy, she's crazy, I'm not messing with her. No one will mess with you.*

The Fantastic Four were humans first. They were four humans, Reed, Sue, Johnny and Ben, who were particularly devoted to their country. They took it upon themselves to try to beat the Russians in the space race, but when building the ship they failed to consider the effect the atmosphere's cosmic rays would have on it, let alone on their own bodies. When the ship crash-landed they all had *fantastic* abilities: Reed, to stretch (Mr. Fantastic!) and Johnny , to burst into flames (The Human Torch!). It's the last two, Sue and Ben, that I find particularly interesting. Sue now had the ability to become invisible (Invisible Girl), and Ben was transformed into an orange monster with incredible strength (The Thing). Even though the four pledged to use their power to help mankind, there's something about Ben and Sue that feels different. Initially, Invisible Girl's ability is useful for intellectual purposes but also seems like the highest form of self protection—to disappear. And Ben, The Thing, loses all recognizable human features, making him distinctly different from the others. The transformation leaves him frustrated and hostile. Unlike the other three who can blend into the human race, The Thing can't. He is visibly stuck outside of it, which results in moments of fantastic rage.

"Well maybe they're right! Maybe I am a monster!"

He shouted: told her to leave it alone.

Then people will look at you and think, Oh boy, she's crazy, I'm not messing with her. No one will mess with you.

Sue's difference within the group goes beyond gender: her abilities changed and strengthened over time. Initially, her powers were ridiculous, useless. Even when under the protection of invisibility she could be made visible from someone touching her.

Her power does very little to deter Miracle Man or the Submariner, villains who use her to get to the others.

"Ah! I thought so!! It's a human! An invisible Human!"

"Oh!"

"Stop struggling! No one can escape Prince Namor."

Seeing that her plight is helpless, Sue Storm becomes visible again.

Issue #4 The Sub Mariner.

"Too bad invisible girl!! It won't work! I know you're there!
Become visible! The Miracle Man commands you!!
Ahh! That's more like it!
And you must obey me!! I am your Master!!
Signal the other member of the Fantastic Four!! I shall defeat
them forever, here and now!!"

Like a girl in a trance, Susan Storm aims her small flare pistol into the sky, And…

Issue #3 Miracle Man

In the Submariner's case, Sue's defensive invisibility is active. To be passive, for Sue Storm, is to be visible—to give in to her visibility. Dr. Judith Lewis Herman affirms that though most hypnotic states come about from a place of choice, traumatic trancelike states do not.[iii] Celeste, the nun, even in the joy that she experiences within her disassociated states, complained that they were often "inopportune."

> [T]hey had increased in frequency (occurring about once a week) and duration (lasting anywhere from a few seconds to several minutes) and she felt less able to prevent their onset at inopportune times or to snap herself out of this state when necessary.[iv]

Though a sense of calm can settle on the body, there's also something frustrating in the acknowledgement that what's triggering the response doesn't deserve the response. As in, sometimes it comes from a friendly hand at the center of my back, a misunderstood phrase, or even a moment that requires intense concentration, when I'm just on the brink of figuring something out. In these moments, the more I want the state to end the longer it holds.

There is something to be said here about memory—what we can recall and how we can use it. You don't have to believe me but here's what I can say, that for most events and situations I have a good memory, an ability to remember what is said in a conversation, the gestures someone else makes. Like anyone, there are places where I fail, moments when my experience does not seem to be chronicled or digested by my consciousness. According to Freudian psychoanalysts, consciousness is something passive. We naturally bring experience into our consciousness. It is an effort to keep consciousness and experience separate. Freud uses the example of a beach ball being held underwater, and that once it's under, muscular defenses have to remain to maintain it, because naturally, experience and consciousness want to become one. *It happened so suddenly, all by itself.* Herbert Fingarette and Donnel Stern assert that consciousness might not be as passive as we think. We actually have to coax our consciousness to digest our experience. To, as Stern puts it, "haul up a rock from the bottom." Dissociation is not, in that sense, defensive. It is the personality's last resort, when all other defensive measures have been overwhelmed. *Seeing that her plight is helpless, Sue Storm becomes visible again.* We only know what we can express through language, and its through language that the dissociated pieces can be reconstructed and placed together again, free of trauma and full of a new meaning. Through language we develop the ability to "correctly" process the event, to haul the rock upward. We must, Fingarette says, "conceive consciousness as active, not passive. It is something we 'do.' We are 'doers,' and conscious-ness is the exercise of a skill."ᵛ

Reed: Just as I thought! You have greater powers of invisibility than you suspect, Sue! The problem is... How do you learn to control those powers?

Fantastic Four Issue #22
London, January 2004

Dissociation is the inability to reflect on an experience. I am a secondary source. I have two primary sources.

1. A document saved as "It" that is dated, what I assume to be the day after my assault January 27th, 2004 (which I didn't access until June 28th, 2008). I do not remember writing this despite the fact that I recognize it as my own writing. This document contains physical details that I don't remember and in some cases do not believe. What I wrote gives the sense of flickering in and out. Even then, the events of the night come in the form of questions:

    "Did I choose to sleep through it? Did I really wake up when I felt his fist knock against my jaw? Did I really apologize for the sound my teeth made?"

    Somehow the cosmic rays have altered your atomic structure...

2. A journal entry for the same date with two sentences: "He turned out to be creepy." And, "He wouldn't let me sleep."

The morning after the assault I left his flat and began to head towards school. It didn't seem so bad. It was cold outside. My chin, where he hit me, felt chapped and swollen. I walked past a man in a business suit and he looked at my chin, looked at me. I felt filthy. I wrapped my scarf higher so that it covered my chin. At a crosswalk I pulled ginger from my bag (I don't remember buying this). I peeled back a part of the brown skin and took a bite. It was supposed to be good for indigestion, and I felt nauseous. It was supposed to be good for breath. When I arrived at King's Cross there were twenty or thirty men in business suits staring at the tube map. I joined them. The train wasn't running.

I don't remember this. I have constructed this, pieced it together; an effort even to use the word assault. In my primary resource, the Word document, I wrote "we all looked at the map to try to figure the way to go." The station was closed. I remember I walked to school. I hid in the library for two hours before class started. I didn't want anything to eat. I don't remember class or if anyone commented on my face. *Susan! Look at Susan!*

Dr. Herman is gentle in her approach of dissociation. She makes it clear that it would be surprising if people didn't use similar techniques to reduce their perception of trauma.

"This altered state of consciousness," she says, "might be one of nature's small mercies. Protection against unbearable pain."[vi] *It's really beautiful. Lots of times I don't want to come back.* When I've thought about the assault too much, on days when it's the only thing on my mind, the moment of disengagement isn't noticed but welcome. My muscles become loose and heavy. Whatever enables emotion breaks away and drops somewhere toward the bottom of my body. I feel calm and blank. Thoughts are slippery and don't stay for long. Whatever was upsetting or reminding me is deflected and I can drift easily into a warm and sudden sleep. The downside that Dr. Herman has found is that the more powerful these altered states become, the more difficult it is to process the event preventing the integration necessary for healing. To heal is to bring into words what once existed as non-verbal.

Superheroes can't heal, but can they dissociate? Every day they use the power they have to remember what happened to them. The use of their power alone keeps them present, pushes them back, back, back to that traumatic event.

The Thing's physical form is representative of his trauma, his difference, his extraordinary separation from society. Every time he uses his strength, every time the Human Torch converts himself into flame, every time Mr. Fantastic loosens his body, stretches, shrinks, they are reminded of the atomic rays and the crash. Despite the rage the Thing feels, he will still be the Thing. My brother was forced to confront his attack because of the public nature of it. There is a scar on the back of his head where hair won't grow that everyone asks about. When he walks down the street in a way that assures no one will mess with him, he is reminded of the event. Every time he contorts his face, he does not forget why.

What is painful to associate we dissociate. We restrict our ability to interpret the experience, thereby limiting the experiences we even allow ourselves to have.

Because when it happens, an uppercut, you apologize for the sound your teeth make against each other, for the fact that you only knew the term uppercut and didn't know this, that it felt; that you can say the word without mentioning chin, jaw, friction, quiet. And that he thinks your breath is shallow, and so does not let you slip away anymore (Of course you can remember his voice "Your breath is getting shallow"), and wakes you whenever you so blissfully do because he does not want you to die, even though you have decided, just moments ago that it might be preferable. Not self pity, just a simple stirring inside that accepts "I'd rather not" like cheese on top of pasta, a trip to the pool. I'd rather not.

Just as when walking down the street afterwards everyone who looks at you can see through the knitting of the scarf and can run their tongues along that bruise, that swelling. Every man you see knows what has happened and every man you see is suddenly more likely to do it, quicker than before because you are nothing, you are rotting and spoiled. And like that, you are gone. As if time and space were broken and she went off somewhere else. The first moment of leaving the body comes fast as it always will, but soon you will come to depend on it like water in the glass, your mouth to the tap. Lots of times I don't want to come back.

I said, "I'm sorry." I went to sleep. I waited until he left the room to dress. I waited until he came back to leave. I did not fight. You made your point, take my wallet. I walked to the university, I waited in the library for class to start. I went to class. I do not remember class. I apparently wrote a document on my computer and saved it as "It." I remember getting into bed and sleeping for a long time.

"Sue! You've Done it! You created a shield of invisible energy! The radiation from my nuclear measuring device must have increased your power, Sue! But your shield is still too thin! Try to create a stronger one, hon! A thicker shield of invisible energy! Concentrate! That's right!! You're getting it!"

"Oh, Reed… This is Wonderful! Your theory was right! My invisibility is a form of energy, and once I learn to control it, I can turn it into a protective screen!"

Fantastic Four (Issue #33)

If I were a hero I might approach this differently. If I were a hero, this would be the story, the way a Fanboy might tell it: After her assault her mind began functioning in strange and fantastic ways! Not only were most physical moments of the event concealed to her, but she suddenly had the ability to leave her body whenever something threatened her. These bits of information fueled her on a quest for the truth! She used her ability to move deeply, in and out of situations most humans don't have the courage to go.

If I were a hero, that might be how the story would go. The closer I get to the truth, hauling the rock toward the surface, the more I want to pull away from it, drop it. The closer I get to the truth the less I believe it. It's not so bad, I tell myself. It really isn't so bad. There is a difference between the ability and the hero. I am not a hero. There are questions I will refuse to answer.

I have a document entitled "It" that I don't remember writing. I remember a fist against my jaw. I remember him waking me, just as I would fall asleep. I don't know how many times. I don't know what time it was. I don't know how long it lasted. It is unclear what I can believe— if I am the manifestation of that experience. Dissociation is a passive thing, one of nature's small mercies. As if time and space were broken. Like a girl in a trance. Prevents the integration necessary for healing. Feeling her plight is helpless, Sue Storm becomes visible again.

Lester, Rebecca J. Anxious Bliss: A Case Study of Dissociation in a Mexican Nun. *TRANSCULT PSYCHIATRY* 2008; 45; 56

Bradford. Comic Book Nation: The Transformation of Youth Culture in America. Baltimore: Johns Hopkins University Press, 2001.   10

Herman, Judith Lewis. Trauma and Recovery. New York: Basic Books, 1992. 45

Lester. p.57

Stern, Donnel B. Unformulated Experience: From Dissociation to Imagination in Psychoanalysis. Hillsdale, NJ: The Analytic Press, 1997.   85

Herman. 43-45.

CONTRIBUTORS

Hillary Leftwich is a native of Colorado and currently lives in Denver with her son. She is the co-host for At the Inkwell Reading Series in Denver and serves as the associate editor for The Conium Review. Her writing appears in Hobart, Matter Press, NANO Fiction, WhiskeyPaper, Logzplot, Gone Lawn, decomp magazine, Smokelong Quarterly's "Why Flash Fiction?" series, the Review Review's "Views on Publishing," and other journals. She has a chapbook of poems forthcoming from Mutiny Info Press in 2017.

Prerna Bakshi is a two-time Pushcart Prize nominee and the author of Burnt Rotis, With Love, a debut full-length collection of poetry from Les Éditions du Zaporogue (Denmark), long-listed for the 2015 Erbacce-Press Poetry Award in the UK and cited as one of the '9 Poetry Collections That Will Change The Way You See The World' by Bustle Magazine in the US. Her work has been published widely, most recently in The Ofi Press, Red Wedge Magazine, TRIVIA: Voices of Feminism and Prachya Review: Literature & Art Without Borders. More here: http://prernabakshi.strikingly.com/

Mila Jaroniec is the author of *Plastic Vodka Bottle Sleepover* (Split Lip Press, 2016). She is the editor of drDOCTOR and her work has appeared in Playboy, LENNY, Hobart, Joyland, Catapult and Vol. 1 Brooklyn, among others. She lives in Ohio with her partner and son.

Lauren Samblanet is a poet who is working on her m.f.a. at temple university. she is also a writer for thinking dance. her poems have been published in the vassar review, walkabout and adanna, and a dance-radio collaboration with skye hughes was published on colorado public radio's website.

Erin Taylor is an American writer. Her writing often deals with her own experiences and trauma. It is usually poetry, with some exceptions. She has a chapbook of poetry *OOOO* out through Bottlecap Press and she's the interviews editor over at Maudlin House. She is writing a book on loneliness. Her work can be found at erintaylor.tumblr.com and she tweets at @erinisaway.

Stephen Furlong is a graduate student at Southeast Missouri State University located on the Mississippi river. His abuse, at the hands of an older male cousin, happened five times over a three-year period. His current creative project is a manuscript of poetry following the abuse as lensed by the five stages of grief. In addition to receiving nomination for Best New Poets 2016, his poetry and reviews have appeared or are forthcoming in the Chariton Review, Open Minds Quarterly, and Big Muddy, among others.

Lillian Ann Slugocki, founder of BEDLAM, has been nominated twice for the Best of the Web, a Pushcart Prize, and winner of the Gigantic Sequins prize for fiction. She's been published by Seal Press, Cleis Press, Heinemann Press, Newtown Press, Spuyten Duyvil Press, as well as Bloom/The Millions, Salon, Beatrice, THE FEM Literary Magazine, HerKind/Vida, Deep Water Literary Journal, The Nervous Breakdown, The Dr. T.J. Eckleburg Review, Blue Fifth Review, Non Binary Review, The Manifest-Station, Angels Flight * literary west, Entropy, Volume 1 Brooklyn, Sweatpants and Coffee, and The Daily Beast. She has an MA from NYU in literary theory, and has produced and written for Off-Broadway and National Public Radio. How to Travel With Your Demons, a novella, Spuyten Duyvil Press, 2015, chosen for the Doctor T.J. Eckleburg Book Club. Her other books are The Blue Hours, and The Erotica Project, co-author, Erin Cressida Wilson. Anthologies include Wreckage of Reason 2: Back to the Drawing Board and Dirty Girls.

Sloane Eliot Mariem is a Florida-raised, Brooklyn-based poet exploring trauma, recovery, and the formation of new relationships in the wake of domestic violence. Her work has appeared in Vending Machine Press, Calamity, Electric Cereal, and is forthcoming in The Fem. She has read in NYC as part of the Vapors reading series.

Maggie Queeney reads and writes in Chicago. Her work can be found in Copper Nickel, TYPO, Southern Poetry Review, The Southeast Review, and Conjunctions.

Christopher Morgan is a Lebanese American prose poet who grew up in Detroit, the Bible Belt of Georgia, and the San Francisco Bay Area, where he currently lives and co-manages *Nostrovia! Press*. The Reviews Coordinator at *Alien Mouth*, and the author of two chapbooks, "Shadow Songs" (*Sad Spell Press* 2015) and "Fables with Fangs" (*Ghost City Press* 2016), he loves hiking in the redwoods, aphorisms, and happy hour margaritas.

Geula Geurts is a Dutch born poet living in Jerusalem. She completed her MFA in Poetry at Bar Ilan University. Her mini-chapbook "Like Any Good Daughter" is forthcoming with Platypus Press. Further work has appeared or is forthcoming in Tinderbox Editions, Rogue Agent, Hermeneutic Chaos, Cactus Heart, Minerva Rising, The Fem and Jellyfish Review. She works as a Foreign Rights Agent at The Deborah Harris Literary Agency.

Sarah Lilius is the author of the chapbooks What Becomes Within (ELJ Editions, 2014) and The Heart Factory (Black Cat Moon Press, 2016). She has a chapbook forthcoming from Dancing Girl Press early next year. Some of her journal publication credits include the Denver Quarterly, Bluestem, Tinderbox, Hermeneutic Chaos, Stirring, Melancholy Hyperbole, Entropy, and Flapperhouse. She lives in Arlington, VA with her husband and two sons. Her website is sarahlilius.com.

Omotara James resides in New York City, where she is an MFA candidate. She is the recipient of Slice magazine's 2016 Bridging the Gap Award for Emerging Poets, as well as the Nancy P. Schnader Academy of American Poets Award. Her work has appeared or is forthcoming in Winter Tangerine, Visceral Brooklyn, The Coil, Gnosis, Font, and The Anthology of Young American Poets. She has received scholarships from Cave Canem, the Homeschool and the Garrison Institute. Currently, she is an editor at Visceral Brooklyn and Art of Dharma. You can find out what she's doing next at https://omotara-james-poet.squarespace.com

Lauren Milici is a Jersey-born, Florida-bred gal who believes the best art is derived from naked honesty. She is currently pursuing an MFA in Poetry at West Virginia University. She posts drafts, sketches, and other trash on her website, laurenemilici.com.

Shannon Elizabeth Hardwick received her MFA from Sarah Lawrence College. Her first full-length book, Before Isadore, is forthcoming from Sundress Publications. She serves as the poetry editor for The Boiler Journal. Her work has appeared or is forthcoming in the following: Salt Hill, Stirring, Versal, The Texas Observer, Devil's Lake, Four Way Review, among others. Hardwick also has chapbooks out with Thrush Press and Mouthfeel Press.

Stephanie Valente lives in Brooklyn, NY. She has published Hotel Ghost (Bottlecap Press, 2015) and has work included in or forthcoming from Danse Macabre, Nano Fiction, and Black Heart. Sometimes, she feels human. http://stephanievalente.com

Isobel O'Hare is a Pushcart-nominated poet and essayist who has dual Irish and American citizenship. O'Hare is the author of the chapbooks *Wild Materials* (Zoo Cake Press, 2015) and *The Garden Inside Her* (Ladybox Books, 2016). She is based in Oakland, California and Taos, New Mexico.

Shevaun Brannigan is a graduate of the Bennington Writing Seminars, as well as The Jiménez-Porter Writers' House at The University of Maryland. Her poems have appeared in such journals as Best New Poets 2012, Rhino, Redivider, and Crab Orchard Review. She is the first place recipient of the 2015 Jan-ai Scholarship through the Winter Poetry and Prose Getaway, and a 2015 recipient of a Barbara Deming Memorial Fund grant. Also in 2015, she was shortlisted for the Booth Poetry Prize, was a finalist for the District Lit Poetry Prize, a finalist for The Tishman Review's Edna St. Vincent Millay Poetry Prize, and received an honorable mention in The Feminist Wire's inaugural poetry prize. Her work can be found at shevaunbrannigan.com.

Amy Jo Trier-Walker lives and works on a tree and herb farm in Indiana and is the author of two chapbooks: *Trembling Ourselves into Trees* (Horse

Less Press, 2015) and *One Winter Night in the Pines* (The Dandelion Review, 2016). She is the winner of the 2016 Permafrost New Alchemy Contest, and her work can be found in New American Writing, Caliban online, Salt Hill, Tupelo Quarterly, and inter|rupture, among others.

Marty Cain is a poet and video artist. His first book is a long poem called *Kids of the Black Hole* (Trembling Pillow Press, 2017). His work has appeared (or is forthcoming) in *Fence, Jacket2, Tarpaulin Sky, Action Yes, Gigantic Sequins*, and other journals. He received an MFA from the University of Mississippi, and presently, is pursuing a PhD in English Literature at Cornell University. Currently, he lives in Ithaca, New York with his partner, the poet Kina Viola; together, they run Garden-Door Press.

Jennifer Maritza McCauley is a writer, teacher and Ph.D. candidate in creative writing at the University of Missouri. She is also an editorial assistant at The Missouri Review, a reviews editor at Fjords Review and an associate editor of Origins Literary Journal. Her most recent work appears or is forthcoming in editions of The Los Angeles Review, Jabberwock Review, LunaLuna, Split this Rock's "Poem of the Week," Puerto del Sol, The Feminist Wire and New Delta Review, among other outlets.

Alaina Leary is a Bostonian publishing professional. She serves as a social media assistant for the nonprofit We Need Diverse Books. Her work has been published in Cosmopolitan, Seventeen, Marie Claire, Bustle, Bust, Everyday Feminism, The Establishment, and more. When she's not reading, you can usually find her spending time with her two cats or covering everything in glitter.

Alexis Groulx's work has been previously published, or is forthcoming in Blue Lyra Review, Bridge Eight, Gravel, Off the Coast,Sun & Sandstone,The Missing Slate and others.

Patty Paine is the author of Grief & Other Animals (Accents Publishing) The Sounding Machine (Accents Publishing), Feral (Imaginary Friend Press), and co-editor of Gathering the Tide: An Anthology of Contemporary Arabian Gulf Poetry (Ithaca Press) and The Donkey Lady and Other Tales from the Arabian Gulf (Berkshire). Her poems, reviews, and interviews have appeared in Blackbird, Gulf Stream, The

Journal, The South Dakota Review, and other publications. She is the founding editor of Diode Poetry Journal, and Diode Editions, and is Director of Liberal Arts & Sciences at Virginia Commonwealth University, Qatar.

Abigail Welhouse is the author of Bad Baby (dancing girl press), Too Many Humans of New York(Bottlecap Press), and Memento Mori (a poem/comic collaboration with Evan Johnston). Her writing has been published in The Toast, The Billfold, Ghost Ocean Magazine, the Heavy Feather Review, and elsewhere. Subscribe to her Secret Poems at tinyletter.com/welhouse.

Stephanie Berger is the founder and CEO of The Poetry Society of New York, a 501(c)3 dedicated to promoting poetry within our culture. She is the creator and Madame of The Poetry Brothel, co-founder and director of The New York City Poetry Festival, and co-creator of The Typewriter Project. Her poetry has appeared in Fence, The Volta, Hyperallergic, Prelude, Bat City Review, and H_NGM_N, among other publications. She published a chapbook of poems, In The Madame's Hat Box (Dancing Girl Press, 2011) and is the co-author/translator of The Grey Bird (Coconut Books, 2014). She received her MFA in Poetry from The New School and has taught in the English department at Pace University.

Jacklyn Janeksela is a wolf and a raven, a cluster of stars, & a direct descent of the divine feminine. jacklyn janeksela can be found @ Thought Catalog, Luna Magazine, Talking Book, Three Point Press, DumDum Magazine, Visceral Brooklyn, Anti-Heroin Chic, Public Pool, Reality Hands, Mannequin Haus, Velvet-Tail, Requited Journal, The Feminist Wire, Word For/Word, Literary Orphans, Lavender Review, & Pank. she is in a post-punk band called the velblouds. her baby @ femalefilet. more art @ artmugre & a clip. her first book, fitting a witch//hexing the stitch, will be born in 2017 (The Operating System). she is an energy. find her @ hermetic hare for herbal astrological readings.

Christine Stoddard is a Salvadoran-Scottish-American writer and artist who lives in Brooklyn. Her writings have appeared in Marie Claire, The Feminist Wire, Bustle, Teen Vogue, The Huffington Post, Ravishly, So to Speak, Jimson Weed, and beyond. In 2014, Folio Magazine named er one of the top 20 media visionaries in their 20s for founding Quail Bell Magazine. Christine is the author of Hispanic & Latino Heritage in Virginia (The History Press, 2016) and Ova (Dancing Girl Press, 2017.)

Nicole McCarthy is an experimental writer/artist in the MFA program at the University of Washington Bothell. She is also the managing editor of *The James Franco Review*. Her work has appeared in *Punctuate Magazine, The Fem, Ghost Proposal, FLAPPERHOUSE, Crab Fat Magazine, PUBLIC POOL, Tinderbox Poetry,* and others. She is working on her first full-length hybrid collection.

Lynn Melnick is the author of *Landscape with Sex and Violence* (forthcoming, 2017) and *If I Should Say I Have Hope* (2012), both with YesYes Books, and the co-editor of Please Excuse This Poem: 100 New Poets for the Next Generation (Viking, 2015). She serves on the Executive Board of VIDA: Women in Literary Arts.

Ashley Miranda is a latinx poet from Chicago. Her work has been previously featured in The Denver Quarterly, White Stag, pioneertown, and HOUND lit. She tweets impulse poetry and other ramblings @dustwhispers.

Leza Cantoral is editor of CLASH Media Books and Luna Luna Magazine Print Projects. She is the author of 'Cartoons in the Suicide Forest' published by Bizarro Pulp Press. She lives in New Hampshire with the love of her life and their two cats.

Corinne Manning manages the distinction between desire and longing by wearing wigs while chopping wood on a farm in the PNW. While currently at work on a novel about a queer family in post-Columbine America, Corinne has a collection, WE HAD NO RULES, flirting with presses; stories from which have appeared in Story Quarterly, Calyx, Vol 1 Brooklyn, Moss, and The Bellingham Review. "Primary Sources" originally appeared in Arts & Letters and is the first piece of writing that freed and transformed Corinne in its production. Once Upon A Time, Corinne founded a journal called The James Franco Review, dedicated to the visibility of underrepresented artists through reimagining the publishing process.

CAConrad's childhood included selling cut flowers along the highway for his mother and helping her shoplift. The author of 9 books of poetry and essays, the latest is titled *While Standing In Line For Death* and is forthcoming from Wave Books (September 2017). He is a Pew Fellow and has also received fellowships from Lannan Foundation, MacDowell Colony, Headlands Center for the Arts, Banff, RADAR, Flying Ojbect and Ucross. For his books, essays, and details on the documentary *The Book of Conrad* (Delinquent Films 2016), please visit CAConrad.blogspot.com

Danielle Perry graduated with a degree in English Lit and Religious Studies from Guilford College in Greensboro, NC. She now lives in Portland, OR, but will never lose her East Coast charm. She spends probably too much time on Twitter (@jekyllian). Her work has been published in The Toast, FLAPPERHOUSE, and Potluck Magazine, among others. Her chapbook Phases (2015) was published by Sad Spell Press.

Annie Virginia teaches English to high schoolers. She earned her degree in poetry and street vigilantism at Sarah Lawrence College. She worries people by fighting in public with men who need to be fought. Her work was nominated for a Pushcart prize by Broad! magazine and can be found in The Literary Bohemian, Arsenic Lobster, The Legendary, and "The Queer South" by Sibling Rivalry Press.

Claudia Cortese is a poet, essayist, and fiction writer. Her first book WASP QUEEN (Black Lawrence Press, 2016), explores the privilege and pathology, trauma and brattiness of suburban girlhood. Her work has appeared in Blackbird, Black Warrior Review, Crazyhorse, Gulf Coast Online, and The Offing, among others. The daughter of Neapolitan immigrants, Cortese grew up in Ohio and lives in New Jersey. She also lives at claudia-cortese.com

Kelley O'Brien is a disabled lesbian currently studying social work. She enjoys working in her garden and making jewelry, and hopes to make a little difference in the world.

Jessica Lynn Suchon is a poet, essayist, and women's rights advocate. She is currently an MFA candidate at Southern Illinois University. Her work has appeared or is forthcoming in Radar Poetry, decomP, and Rust

+ Moth, among others. In 2016, she was named an Emerging Writer Fellow by Aspen Words, a partner of the Aspen Institute. She currently lives and writes in Carbondale, Illinois with her boyfriend Josh Myers and their dog Gracie.

Hannah Kucharzak is a poet and visual artist from Chicago. Her poems have been previously published in TYPO, Vagabond City, Requited, Pleiades, Pinwheel, Ghost Proposal, and elsewhere. She is the recipient of the Gwendolyn Brooks Award and the Luminarts Award for Creative Writing.

Sarah Madges is a Brooklyn-based writer with an MFA from The New School Creative Writing Program. She co-curates Handwritten, an online project dedicated to the art and act of handwriting, and runs the monthly poetry reading series, Mental Marginalia. Her writing has appeared in The Village Voice, Killing the Angel, SCOUT: Poetry in Review, and elsewhere.

Staci R. Schoenfeld is a recipient of a 2015 NEA Fellowship for Poetry. She's a PhD student at University of South Dakota and assistant editor for poetry at South Dakota Review. Recent poems appear in Mid-American Review, Southern Humanities Review, and Thrush Poetry Journal. Her chapbook, The Patient Admits, is forthcoming from dancing girl press in summer 2017.

Alexis Smithers is a queer black writer on the East Coast. Their work can be found in wusgood.black, Glass: Poetry, and Up the Staircase Quarterly and forthcoming in &thriving among others. They work for Monstering Mag, Winter Tangerine Review, Words Dance, and Voicemail Poems. They are a 2015 Pink Door Fellow and 2016 LAMBDA Literary Emerging Writers Fellow. A full list of their work can be found at lexleecom.wordpress.com.

Agnes Vittstrand is a nom de guerre, a feminist activist and author of "Allt som tar plats" (FRF, 2014) a collection of poems on strategies built after having her childhood broken by pedophiles. She has published articles in numerous Swedish feminist magazines and is also a painter of some astute. Her next book is in line for publishing by anarchist press Freke Räihä Förlag.

Freke Räihä is an elderly queer poet, translator and literary curator with more issues than vowels.

Jason Phoebe Rusch is a queer, non-binary writer from the Chicago suburbs. They have a BA in history from Princeton University and an MFA in fiction from University of Michigan, where they were a Zell Fellow and received several Hopwood awards. Their poetry has appeared in Luna Luna, their essays in Bust magazine, World Policy Journal online and The Mighty and their screenplay Banana Rat was a finalist in the 2010 Zoetrope contest.

Leah Mueller is an independent writer from Tacoma, Washington. She is the author of one chapbook, "Queen of Dorksville", and two full-length books, "Allergic to Everything" and "The Underside of the Snake." Her work has been published or is forthcoming in Blunderbuss, Memoryhouse, Outlook Springs, Atticus Review, Sadie Girl Press, Origins Journal, Silver Birch Press, Cultured Vultures, Quail Bell, and many others. She was a featured poet at the 2015 New York Poetry Festival and a runner-up in the 2012 Wergle Flomp Humor Poetry contest.

MW Murphy is a poet and novelist. She is the author of the novel Second Daughter, which was endorsed with cover blurbs by best-selling author Wally Lamb as well as cult author and Yale professor John Crowley. Second Daughter was subsequently picked by NPR's Faith Middleton as a "shelf-tracker" book of the month, and was also a featured book at R J Julia Booksellers. MW was selected for publication several times in the "Open Weave" poetry anthology published by Curbstone Press / Northwestern University, which also awarded her first place in its Poet Laureate Division. She has a short piece of fiction in the anthology Gathered Light which was published by Three O' Clock Press in May 2013. MW also has recent poems in the international poetry anthology series "The Art of Being Human – Volume 13, Volume 14, and Volume 15", all of which were published in 2015. She is currently nearing completion of an urban sci/fi fantasy novel which takes place mostly in Manhattan's East Village.

Katie Clark is a queer poet & a sophomore at Mount Holyoke. Katie's poems have been in several kind publications including Nostrovia! and Voicemail Poems. Tweets @octupiwallst

Christoph Paul is an award-winning humor author. He writes non-fiction, YA, Bizarro, horror, and poetry including: The Passion of the Christoph, Great White House Volume 1 and Volume 2, Slasher Camp for Nerd Dorks, and Horror Film Poems. He is an editor for CLASH Media and CLASH Books and edited the anthologies Walk Hand in Hand Into Extinction: Stories Inspired by True Detective and This Book Ain't Nuttin to Fuck With: A Wu-Tang Tribute Anthology. Under the pen name Mandy De Sandra, he writes Bizarro Erotica that has been covered in VICE, Huffington Post, Jezebel, and AV Club. He is represented by Veronica Park at Corvisiero Literary Agency.

Lauren Davis is a poet living on the Olympic Peninsula where she works as an editor for The Tishman Review. She holds an MFA from the Bennington Writing Seminars, and her work can be found in journals such as Prairie Schooner, Spillway, and Clarion.

Lora Nouk is a New York-based artist and poet. She works across various mediums including net art, performance, BJD and text. She has presented work at Picture Room, New York; Kodomo/Manila Institute, Brooklyn; Mellow Pages, Brooklyn; MoMA PS1, New York; and David Lewis Gallery, New York, among others. She is the author of Snow Poems (Codette, 2015). She tweets @shad0w_paws

Diane Payne's most recent publications include: Map Literary Review, Watershed Review, Tishman Review, Whiskey Island, Kudzu House Quarterly, Superstition Review, Burrow Press,Dime Show Review, Lime Hawk, and Cheat River Review. She has work forthcoming in The Offing, Elke: A little Journal, Souvenir Literary Journal, Outpost 19. Diane is the author of Burning Tulips (Red Hen Press) and is the MFA Director at University of Arkansas at Monticello.

EDITOR

Joanna C. Valente is a human who lives in Brooklyn, New York. They are the author of Sirs & Madams (Aldrich Press, 2014), The Gods Are Dead (Deadly Chaps Press, 2015), Marys of the Sea (2016, ELJ Publications) & Xenos (2016, Agape Editions). They received their MFA in writing at Sarah Lawrence College. Joanna is also the founder of Yes, Poetry, as well as the managing editor for Civil Coping Mechanisms and Luna Luna Magazine. Some of their writing has appeared in Prelude, BUST, The Atlas Review, The Feminist Wire, The Huffington Post, Columbia Journal, and elsewhere. Joanna also leads workshops at Brooklyn Poets.

OFFICIAL

CCM ●

GET OUT OF JAIL
* VOUCHER *

- -

Tear this out.
Skip that social event.
It's okay.
You don't have to go if you don't want to. Pick up
the book you just bought. Open to the first page.
You'll thank us by the third paragraph.

If friends ask why you were a no-show, show them
this voucher.
You'll be fine.

- -

We're coping.

●

CPSIA information can be obtained
at www.ICGtesting.com
Printed in the USA
LVOW11s0121160817
545172LV00002B/202/P